PLAYBOATING THE
NANTAHALA RIVER

AN ENTRY LEVEL GUIDE

Including a Section on
the Tuckaseigee River Gorge

Kelly Fischer

Illustrated by
Keith Calhoun

milestone
press

almond, nc

Milestone Press, P.O. Box 158, Almond, NC 28702

Cover and book design by TO Design, Asheville, NC

Cover photos by Carlos Steward, courtesy of the Nantahala Outdoor Center

Library of Congress Cataloging-in-Publication Data

Fischer, Kelly, 1966-

   Playboating the Nantahala River ; an entry level guide : including a section on the Tuckaseigee River Gorge / Kelly Fischer ; illustrated by Keith Calhoun.

        p. cm.

     Includes bibliographical references (p.).

     ISBN 1-889596-05-1

     1. White-water canoeing—Nantahala River (N.C.)—Guidebooks. 2. Kayaking—Nantahala River (N.C.)—Guidebooks. 3. Nantahala River (N.C.)—Guidebooks.   I. Title.

GV776.N74F57 1998

797.1′22′097568—dc21   98-10272

                                                              CIP

This publication is sold with the understanding that the author and publisher assume no legal responsibility for the completeness or accuracy of the contents of this book, nor for any damages incurred while attempting any of the moves described within it. The text is based on information available at the time of publication. River rapids and other features are subject to change at any time, and whitewater paddling is a sport with inherent risks. This book is not intended as a replacement for proper instruction or adequate skill level. Each paddler must assess his or her own abilities before attempting to run any river or rapid.

Printed on recycled paper in the United States of America.

Acknowledgments

I am grateful to the following people who helped me complete this guidebook. Without them, it would be far from finished.

If a picture is worth a thousand words, Keith Calhoun's illustrations have saved me a million. A skilled canoeist, Keith has brought the rapids to life in both *A Playboater's Guide to the Ocoee River* and *Playboating the Nantahala River*. If you look closely, you can see him disguised as the radical open boater in many of the drawings.

Will Leverette was a great help in writing the history pages and many of the anecdotes. The grandson of the late western North Carolina paddling legend Frank Bell, Will grew up with the history of Nantahala paddling. A series of articles on the history of the Nantahala by George Ellison which appeared in *The Asheville Citizen Times* in 1992 also provided historical information about the Nantahala Gorge.

Payson and Aurelia Kennedy, Bunny Johns, John Burton and Horace Holden, Sr., all of whom were around from the early days of recreational paddling on the Nantahala, helped to fill in many historical details and verify dates. The NOC raft guide training manual, written by Ray McLeod, was also a valuable resource, as was the Nantahala Racing Club.

Contents

Introduction

Whitewater paddling has come of age. Boaters no longer use kayaks and canoes strictly as a means to descend a scenic river. Over the years, an explosion has occurred in the facet of the sport we now call playboating. Playboaters travel to very specific whitewater locations to practice and perfect their repertoire of advanced skills and acrobatic stunts.

To become a skilled playboater, a paddler progresses through a number of increasingly difficult river-running skills leading to that goal. The ability to cross eddy lines efficiently and paddle through rapids under control are critical building blocks on the way to mastering cartwheels, pirouettes and other advanced playboating stunts. This guidebook will help developing boaters find the best places on the Nantahala and Tuckaseigee Rivers to practice the fundamental skills that will propel them down the playboating path.

Whitewater rodeos are increasing in popularity at a dramatic rate. Rodeos are whitewater events held at popular play spots on various rivers across the country—and internationally—where playboaters congregate and compete against one another. Many newcomers to the sport are introduced to canoeing and kayaking as spectators, and aspire to be rodeo stars before they ever get interested in running rivers.

Of course, not everybody wants to be a rodeo star, but playboating moves are now integral to the sport. Most paddlers on the river today can tell you the difference between a McTwist and a Split Wheel. Many boaters who have been paddling for a long time are trading in their longer river-running boats for short playboats designed specifically to do whitewater stunts.

Each year, thousands of people come to the Nantahala region to learn to paddle and improve their playboating skills. With warm weather that begins early in the spring and extends late into the fall, the Nantahala and the Tuckaseigee rivers are premier choices for nearly year-round paddling, and consistent dam releases on both ensure good water levels.

No river in the world has introduced more paddlers to

whitewater than the Nantahala. It offers textbook-quality river features—Class II and III rapids, eddy lines perfect for honing eddy turns and peel-out skills, jets of current slow enough for the most cautious novice and fast enough to challenge the advanced paddler, and waves of all sizes and types. Surfing holes and ender spots can keep a developing playboater busy all day. There's even a world-class whitewater slalom training site at the take-out. If this isn't enough to hook you, the clear water and the beauty of the river gorge itself surely will be.

The Tuckaseigee is a great option for avoiding some of the crowds the Nantahala can attract, and the water is substantially warmer. This makes it an excellent choice for folks working on whitewater Eskimo rolls. The "Tuck," with its Class I and II rapids, is a great first river where novices can enjoy a more relaxed introduction to whitewater.

This book is divided into a number of different parts. First, the fundamental concepts section is a reminder of the basic elements of technique. Next, you'll find the rapids of the Nantahala and the Tuckaseigee. The individual play spots are broken down, described and illustrated in detail, and direct routes through rapids are given for times when you want to run the rapid without stopping to play. Following this is an alternate put-in section for the Nantahala, which is helpful if you want to paddle small sections of the river at a time and work them more completely. Finally, a glossary of terms is provided to help you sound more hip in an experienced crowd.

This guide is not meant to replace quality instruction. It's a tool to enhance your learning experience after formal paddling classes are over and you venture out on your own. Decide what aspects of whitewater boating most appeal to you and which skills you want to improve. Set realistic goals. Scan through the book to find the best locations to practice, remember your fundamentals and then safely go after those goals. This book is sized so you can take it on the river—so stuff it in a dry bag and go.

K.F.
April, 1998

A Short History of Nantahala Whitewater

The Nantahala River flows through a steep, narrow gorge 15 miles east of Bryson City, North Carolina. The river was a peaceful, remote trout stream before Nantahala Power & Light built the hydroelectric power plant which began operation in 1942. Today, nearly 250,000 people a year use it for recreational whitewater paddling. Although the water comes out of the bottom of Nantahala Lake at a chilly 45°, this river is one of the best in the country for learning and perfecting whitewater paddling skills.

It is not known exactly who first ran the Nantahala in a canoe. The late Frank Bell, who was credited with many first descents in the Southern Appalachians, told Payson Kennedy that it was probably Ramone Eaton. Eaton was a friend and fellow pioneer who contributed greatly to the development of whitewater paddling, primarily through his involvement with the strong canoeing programs of western North Carolina's summer camps.

In 1943, a small group from Camp Mondamin in Tuxedo, NC, ran the river in wooden canoes. Bell, who was the camp's owner, and Eaton led the trip. With much scouting, they managed to run the river in 10 hours without serious problems and only one near miss. Although they portaged Nantahala Falls, one canoe almost washed over Wesser Falls.

For the next 30 or so years, recreational paddling on the Nantahala and other area rivers was undertaken by a relatively small circle of enthusiasts, the nucleus of which was the strong whitewater programs of four area summer camps—Mondamin, Green Cove, Merrie-Woode, and High Rocks. In 1972, the Nantahala Outdoor Center was founded by Payson and Aurelia Kennedy and Horace Holden, Sr. The following year, the movie *Deliverance* thrust whitewater paddling into the collective consciousness of the American public.

After the Second World War, aluminum began to replace wood and canvas when Grumman Aircraft started producing canoes. The first fiberglass boat, probably a C-1 paddled by David Williams, appeared on the river in 1965. In 1973, the Blue Hole Canoe Company put into production the first Royalex ABS canoe, and several companies started making plastic kayaks. The public, which now had access to rubber rafts and more durable boats that were easier to paddle, began to arrive in droves. The US Forest Service reports that about 241,500 individuals paddled the river in 1996. Of those, an estimated 31,500 were private boaters.

In 1969, the Georgia Canoe Association held the area's first open canoe race on the Nantahala. Since then, it has been the site of many regional, national and international competitions. Over the decades, slalom, wildwater and triathlon races, and national team trials have all been held on this river, as well as Nantahala '90, an international raft rally which hosted 240 athletes representing 17 countries. The river is now home to the Nantahala Racing Club, which is one of the country's most important racing development programs and a Whitewater Center of Excellence designated by the US Canoe and Kayak Team.

As whitewater sport has evolved, our estimation of the difficulty of the rivers we run has changed, and the Nantahala is no exception. Perhaps one of the most telling facts about the development of paddling technology and technique is that Nantahala Falls was once rated a Class V rapid. Today, that same rapid is considered a textbook example of Class III whitewater.

In the 1967 edition of his *Canoeing Whitewater: A Guidebook,* Randy Carter described the river as "all an open canoe can handle," and cautioned that the Falls "should be attempted only by experts." Today, the Nantahala is the first introduction to whitewater for many beginners, and novice-to-intermediate paddlers often run the Falls successfully in canoes and kayaks. That's quite a jump from the wood and canvas canoe era of the 1940s, when paddling the Nantahala meant riding the cutting edge of adventure.

None of this diminishes, however, the beauty and classic qualities of the Nantahala itself. For many paddlers, novice and expert alike, it remains, as Randy Carter put it, "the most delightful canoeing river of all."

River Information

Locating the Rivers

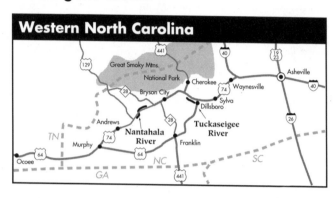

The **Nantahala River** is located in far western North Carolina between the towns of Bryson City and Andrews. It runs right alongside US Highway 19/74, flowing from west to east. The section of the **Tuckaseigee River** described in this book is located just west of Dillsboro and runs parallel to US 74, with the take-out at Tuckaseegee Outfitters. It flows from east to west. It takes just over half an hour to drive from the Nantahala take-out to the Tuckaseigee put-in and vice versa.

Information & Resources

These are the numbers to call for information about where to stay, what the river is doing, other activities available in the river corridor, and generally any questions you may have about the Nantahala and Tuckaseigee rivers and the surrounding area. Please note that until June 1998, the area code for these numbers is 704.

Smoky Mountain Host	828/369-9606
Bryson City Chamber of Commerce	800/867-9246
Nantahala Outdoor Center	828/488-2175
Tuckaseegee Outfitters	828/586-5050
Nantahala Power & Light	828/369-4556

Water Levels on the Nantahala

The release level considered normal on the Nantahala is 586 cubic feet per second (cfs), and rarely does the flow vary from that norm. During periods of drought, Nantahala Power and Light (NP&L) will decrease the level somewhat. Occasionally, the release will be higher, and the river also flows higher due to natural runoff during periods of high rainfall. Most of the river features described in this book remain the same between lower and normal (586 cfs) flow, while at higher levels a few spots get better and a few others are eliminated entirely.

Water Levels on the Tuckaseigee

Releases on the Tuckaseigee can vary slightly depending on which of the four upstream dams is releasing the water. Currently, water is released strictly "on demand" for power generation. Through the warmer months you can expect fairly consistent flows, but just to be sure, you may want to call Tuckaseegee Outfitters or the Nantahala Outdoor Center before heading out.

Rules of the River

Wear a personal flotation device (PFD) and wear it correctly. This seems like common sense and should go without saying.

Alcohol and paddling do not mix. Wait until after you take out and have run your shuttle to impair your faculties.

Respect the fishermen. Move to the other side of the river.

No littering. Pack out your trash. Also, trash cans are located in various places along the river.

Be mindful of where your park your vehicle. Do not block a popular put-in all day long with your car.

Learn river etiquette. This includes:

- Give the right of way to the boat that most needs it.

- Look upstream before entering a wave or hole and yield the right of way to the boat in the current.

- When arriving at a play spot, check out how the lines work. Then go to the end of one and wait your turn. For example, most people line up on river left at both Surfing Rapid and Nantahala Falls, but some folks will enter from the other side as well. When two lines form, they alternate.

Pay the river use fee. The USFS currently charges $1 per person per day or $5 per person for a season pass. This money stays in the river district to be used for maintaining facilities.

Boating safety reminders.

- You are responsible for your own safety.

- Get good instruction before putting on the river.

- Use good equipment.

- All boats need flotation bags.

- Learn whitewater swimming techniques. Keep those feet up and pointed downstream.

• Never boat alone. Period.

Serious Business:
The Screw-up factor

The **Screw-up factor** system of rating play spots is simply a guideline for assessing the difficulty of the playboating moves described in this book. It is not to be considered the ultimate authority for all paddlers. Some moves are more difficult than others, and play spots have varying degrees of risk associated with them. The Screw-up factor simply encourages you to look at potential consequences and make sound decisions, based on your abilities, about whether or not to use a certain play spot or attempt a particular move there.

This book assumes the user to be at the novice-to-intermediate skill level or above, and familiar with the fundamentals of whitewater boating and safety. To use the book most effectively, you should have at least the beginnings of a reliable roll, good balance, and be able to safely negotiate Class II and III rapids.

The Screw-up factor system works on a scale of 1 to 10. A rating of 1 has the least threatening consequences of not making a move successfully, and a rating of 10 will have very high consequences. Consequences may include banging your head or shoulder on a rock, pinning in a ledge, or merely washing through a wave train. Most play spots in this book are given a rating, along with some description of what can potentially happen. Certainly, not all possibilities could be documented, so if you have screwed up in an interesting, unprecedented way, go ahead and name it after yourself.

Recognize that everyone learns at different speeds. Challenge yourself, but set realistic goals. It's always a drag to see new boaters with an arm in a sling, or worse, because enthusiasm got them into situations they weren't ready for.

Finally, make your own decisions about whether to run a rapid, attempt a hairy ferry or get into a hole. It is poor form to follow other boaters into a situation without thinking it through for yourself. Getting inspiration from others is good; just realize that thinking is a big part of the sport, and when enthusiasm enters the picture, thinking for yourself is doubly important. Don't leave your brain in the car when you put on the river. Take it with you and make thoughtful, informed decisions.

Fundamental Concepts

There are some fundamental concepts common to all river maneuvers. This section is intended as a reminder of these fundamentals.

All paddling maneuvers include position, balance, speed and angle. Whether you're an elite slalom paddler going for the gold in the Olympic Games, a developing rodeo star, or a first-year boater learning to have fun running rivers, the concepts are the same. Spend some time understanding and perfecting these fundamentals, and you'll find your river moves will begin to come a little easier and your shred progression will progress a little faster.

Position

To maximize your odds of successfully completing a move, it's important to begin from the best possible position.

Peel-outs. When performing a peel-out, begin near the eddy line and downstream of the rock creating the eddy. Starting too close to the rock or too deep in the eddy tends to hinder correct angle and speed and make the move more difficult.

Eddy Turns. The same applies for entering an eddy. Begin the move from a good position far upstream of the eddy, allowing time to set your angle and enough space to generate some speed before crossing the eddy line.

Wave surfing. When planning to surf a wave or hole, look for the easiest point of entry. Each play spot will have an entry line that is the easiest. Take a moment to look at the water, watch other paddlers and see the move before attempting it. You'll be surprised at how much this will improve your chances of success.

Balance and Boat Lean

Keeping your boat upright while playboating begins with a good sense of balance. Not everyone is naturally gifted with good balance, but it can be learned. Proper posture and flexibility in the boat are the key ingredients. Sit upright with your pelvis tilted forward slightly and your back straight. Flexibility allows the body maximum effectiveness, especially when doing J-leans, the most often used balance technique in playboating.

J-lean. This technique is used when crossing eddy lines, ferrying, and surfing waves and holes. You can practice a J-lean exercise on flat water. Keep your head and shoulders centered over your hips as you lean the boat on edge. Do not lean your body out over the water. Relax and focus on curving your spine sideways and your head and shoulders should move into place naturally. A general rule is to J-lean into the turn being performed. Lean left while the boat is turning left and lean right while the boat is turning right.

Correct J-lean
(head and shoulders centered over hips)

Incorrect Lean
(body leans out over water)

Speed

The speed of a boat is always relative to the current in which it travels. To make most river moves, you must be able to move the boat faster than the current. The exception is front and back ferrying, when you need to go slower than the current.

Ferries, Peel-outs & Eddy Turns. When doing a ferry, peel-out or eddy turn, use speed across the eddy line to move the boat more quickly, reducing the destabilizing effect of the eddy line. If you have insufficient momentum when you cross the eddy line, your bow and stern are each affected by a different current—the eddy current moving upstream and the main current moving downstream. This often results in the boat spinning on the eddy line and flipping over, so cross that unstable eddy line with some speed.

Anchor the Paddle to Move the Boat

Put the paddle in the water before you pull on it. This may sound like a self-evident concept, but it is commonly ignored. Notice how a skilled paddler can make a move with just a few strokes where others can take nine or ten strokes and then miss the move entirely. Stroke efficiency is a major element in effective playboating.

The first step in a good stroke is the "catch" phase. The paddle enters the water to catch some water resistance. The resistance should feel solid, as if the paddle is anchored in the water. If you pull on the paddle before it makes the initial catch, the stroke is splashy and the boat hardly moves at all. When there's a good catch, the power phase moves the boat forward more effectively and sets you up for the next stroke.

All About Angles

The angle of the boat is always relative to the current and eddy lines. In this book, angle is described in a number of different ways.

Open angle. An open angle is one where the boat is almost perpendicular to the current. It is also called a **radical or piercing angle**. This angle exposes more boat to the current as you cross out of an eddy, resulting in faster, more dynamic turns. In fast current the boat will turn downstream very quickly, making it difficult to control.

Closed angle. A closed angle is when the boat is closer to parallel with the current. This can be called a **conservative or safe angle** when doing peel-outs and ferries. Because very little of the boat is exposed to the current as you cross out of an eddy, this angle allows you more control when crossing eddy lines, resulting in slower turns and fewer flips.

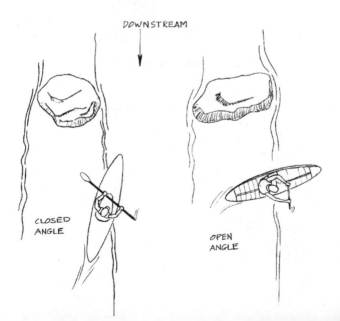

DOWNSTREAM

CLOSED
ANGLE

OPEN
ANGLE

The Nantahala River Rapids

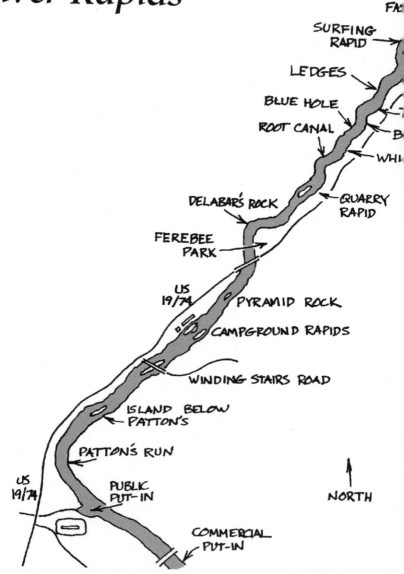

FA...

SURFING RAPID

LEDGES

BLUE HOLE

ROOT CANAL

B...

WHI...

DELABAR'S ROCK

QUARRY RAPID

FEREBEE PARK

US 19/74

PYRAMID ROCK

CAMPGROUND RAPIDS

WINDING STAIRS ROAD

ISLAND BELOW PATTON'S

PATTON'S RUN

US 19/74

PUBLIC PUT-IN

NORTH

COMMERCIAL PUT-IN

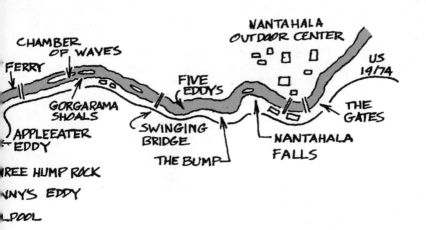

FERRY

CHAMBER
OF WAVES

NANTAHALA
OUTDOOR CENTER

US
19/74

GORGARAMA
SHOALS

FIVE
EDDYS

THE
GATES

APPLEEATER
EDDY

SWINGING
BRIDGE

NANTAHALA
FALLS

THREE HUMP ROCK

THE BUMP

NNY'S EDDY

POOL

Commercial Put-in: About 600 cfs enters the river at the confluence of the natural streambed and the discharge canal for the powerhouse. Both the commercial put-in and the take-out for the upper Nantahala run are located here. Most rafting companies begin their trips at this point, and it is a very busy spot during the peak summer months. On a not-so-busy day it's a good place to warm up with some peel-out practice.

DISCHARGE →

DOWNSTREAM →

PEEL-OUTS

NATURAL BED

Warming up at the commercial put-in

1 **Practice Peel-outs.** As the discharge water passes the point of land separating the natural streambed from the discharge canal, the continuous current creates a well-defined eddy line. Peel out into the current and then recover by going back into the put-in eddy. Try ferry warm-ups here, too. Move out across the current and into the small eddies on the river left shore, then return to the put-in eddy.

Screw-up factor: 6. The risk of flipping in the 45–50° water makes for a higher than average screw-up factor. This water is cold! A flip here can be an unsettling beginning to the day.

A hundred yards downstream is a rapid without a name that's nice for some warm-up ferries. As you enter the rapid you will see that most of the water is moving from left to right into some rocks. Catch the eddy on the left first and then ferry over below where the water is pushing into those rocks. Flipping in this area is no big deal. Self-rescue to the right.

Public Put-in: The put-in is a large eddy at the confluence of the Nantahala and Rowlin Creek. This eddy has enough room to do some warming up before you head out. The exit move from the eddy crosses a fast line of current and can be intimidating if you're not prepared for it. For an easier alternative, just spin around and exit at the bottom of the eddy.

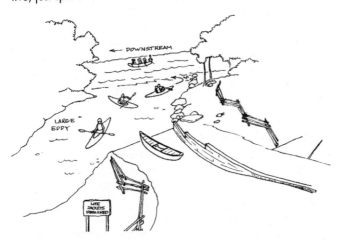

Starting your day at the public put-in

① **Dynamic Peel-out.** If you want to start off with a dynamic peel-out, try moving to the top of the eddy and exiting across the first wave. The wave will give you some exciting acceleration and jet you into the main flow—a great start to your day on the Nantahala.

② **Surfing and Stern Squirts.** Try the second wave for some fun surfing and the eddy line for some good stern squirts. For squirts, cross the eddy line just above the wave with very little speed while watching your stern. Plant your paddle in the eddy water and be sure not to lean your boat upstream until you cross the eddy line.

Screw-up factor: 6. Again, the water is cold. Flipping early on takes the fire out of some paddlers and decides their day immediately. If you do flip, self-rescue to the left and watch for overhanging branches. After peeling out, move to the center of the river. By leaving this eddy, you've committed to running the first big rapid, Patton's Run.

Patton's Run is the first rapid of significance on the Nantahala and the second most difficult rapid of the entire run. It's just around the corner from the put-in, and it comes up fast. If you use the public put-in, there's no warm-up—Patton's Run is your very first rapid.

The river makes a bend to the right, and an overlook on the left bank high above the rapid may be filled with onlookers waiting for you to crash and burn. The best place to scout is from that overlook on your way to the put-in. You can also walk down the trail on the downstream side of the overlook parking area and scout at river level. Many folks use this spot as an alternate put-in, avoiding Patton's Run altogether—good strategy for the inexperienced.

1 Easiest Line. For the most conservative line, round the corner on the inside of the curve and stay right of the main ledge. Crashing through the big wave with left angle will allow you to miss the large rock on the right and continue downstream.

Screw-up factor: 6. That large rock has pinned a few boats, so give it some space and you should slip by without a problem. If you end up floating into the rock sideways, remember to lean toward it, presenting your hull to the current. This should help you slide around it. If your boat gets pinned, do not string a line to the left side of the river on a busy day. If you can't retrieve your boat from river right, wait for more qualified assistance or until the water goes off in the evening.

2 Eddy-hopping. If you're looking for challenges right away, there are a number of eddies to catch here. The sequence begins far upstream of the ledge on river right and moves through ten or so eddies, ending at the ledge on the left side. Control your downstream speed by catching all of the eddies and creeping down to the ledge.

Screw-up factor: 5. It is easy to miss a move and get spun downstream.

3 Wave Surfing. For access to the wave just river right of the ledge, catch the big eddy river left below the ledge. Often it is a crashing wave, almost a hole, and it usually gives fast and dynamic rides, leaving little time to recover into the eddy. To

A lot happens at Patton's Run

get on it, edge sideways to set up next to the eddy line, then cross onto the wave with upstream speed.

Screw-up factor: 4. The water is fast and deep, so roll up immediately and head left for the small eddies on the bank to make your way back up for a second try. Don't work too hard here because you still have over seven miles of river to run.

Patton's Run is named after Charlie Patton, a postman from Brevard, NC, who had suffered a serious injury to one of his arms in World War II. He essentially paddled his canoe (and later his C-1) using only one arm. Charlie was a tireless instructor of beginners, and introduced so many people to the Nantahala that its first major rapid was named in his honor.

Just below the recovery eddies at Patton's Run, the river is divided by a long island. Most people follow the main flow of the water around the right side of the island for good wave-crashing fun. For some solitude and a great warm-up spot, try the left side.

① Current Work To The Left. To the left of the island you'll find a big rock jutting from the left bank with a good eddy behind it. Directly across the river is another good eddy. Spend some time here tuning up your ferrying skills.

Screw-up factor: 3. The current runs deep and is good for rolling practice. Self-rescue is easy; you can go right or left.

② Wave-crashing To The Right. To the right of the island the current is fast and fun. Move across the river to enter the rapid just river right of the center of the channel, then thread your way through the rocky, shallow water at the top until you get past the point of the island where the water picks up speed. Run down the center of the current until it rejoins the left channel and some great waves develop. Crash through the waves and feel the rush.

Screw-up factor: 3-4. The water is fast through this section and the eddies have tree limbs hanging low. If you swim, assume the whitewater position and swim aggressively to shore.

The next half-mile is great water for warming up. The water starts to slow down a bit, so you can catch your breath and begin to set your own pace. Take the opportunity to catch some good eddies in this stretch and practice reading the river.

One of the first European explorers to visit the Nantahala Gorge was William Bartram, a noted Philadelphia naturalist. In May 1775, he met the great Cherokee chief, Ata-Kullakulla, at a location near Patton's Run. There is a historical marker commemorating Bartram's visit on US 19/74 near the Patton's Run pull-off. The foot trail that parallels the river between the commercial put-in and Winding Stairs bridge is a short segment of the Bartram Trail, a long-distance footpath that follows the route of the explorer, beginning in Georgia and finishing atop North Carolina's Cheoah Bald, high above the gorge.

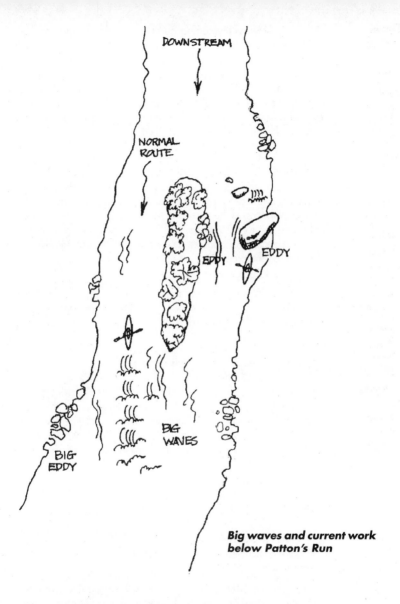

DOWNSTREAM

NORMAL ROUTE

EDDY

EDDY

BIG WAVES

BIG EDDY

Big waves and current work below Patton's Run

25

You'll know the campground rapids are coming up when you pass under Winding Stairs Road, the first bridge over the river. You'll see the long, flat stretch of river bordering the campground on river left. At the end of this stretch is an island split by many channels. The main channel goes straight down the center of the riverbed and is pretty easy. The far right side is shallow and is often choked with tree limbs, so be cautious if you go there. The left channel has some fun eddies to catch.

Peel-out Tune-ups. After passing under the bridge, move left into the campground eddy. Its large size and well-defined eddy line make it perfect for tuning up your peel-outs. Cross the river at the top of the eddy and jet across the first wave, or peel out lower down for an easier move. Once in the current, turn around and head back in for another go, or cross the current again for an eddy turn on the other side.

Screw-up factor: 2. The water is deep at the left eddy line and gets shallow as you move over to the right eddy. If you swim, go in either direction for self-rescue, then empty your boat and head up for another try. This is a great spot to learn some good skills.

Eddy-hopping. The left channel is a fun choice because of the small eddies to catch there. The first eddy is on the right just as you enter the channel. The second is under the bridge on river left and the third one is on the right just after the right-hand bend in the channel. There are still more eddies below the island; try moving across the main channel and into the eddies far river right where the right channel rejoins the main one. There are also some fun attainments to be done going up the right channel.

Screw-up factor: 1-2. This whole area is filled with shallow, slow water, so it's a fun place to bop around.

Wave-busting. Beyond the islands, the current moves left and compresses into a wave train. Line up to run these waves and bust them wide open.

Screw-up factor: 2. Always use the whitewater swimmer's position to get to shore, even in slow-water places like those around the campground.

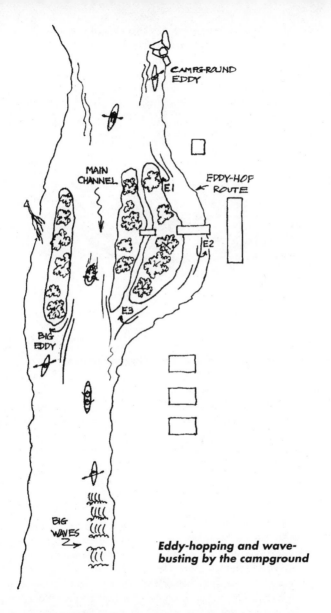

Eddy-hopping and wave-busting by the campground

After a quarter-mile of Class I and II water, you'll come to Pyramid Rock rapid, a great little S-turn rapid easily identified by the large pyramid rock on the left at the very top. There are good eddies to catch here and some great eddy lines for stern squirting.

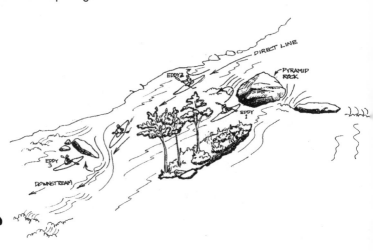

Fun eddies and fast water at Pyramid Rock

① Direct Line. Begin river right and run down the center of the current between Pyramid Rock and the shoreline. Angle left to go past the rock on the right and then stay in the center to get between the large eddies around the left bend.

Screw-up factor: 3. Fast and shallow water absolutely requires swimming in the "safe," or "whitewater," position.

② Eddy-hopping. The first eddy to catch is right behind Pyramid Rock. It is a moving eddy and will push you up against the rock if you aren't careful. Enter it with a fair amount of speed and definitely a good lean, or you'll be upside-down counting the fish here. From behind Pyramid Rock you can move across the fast water to the eddy on the river right shore. Before you go, spend a moment setting your angle correctly because that eddy line is moving fast. An 11 o'clock angle is about right.

From the river right eddy, try moving to the eddy behind the rock in the center of the current just downstream. (Most folks will go back to the pyramid rock eddy for a better set-up to make the center one.) The eddy line is fast here as well. There are more eddies downstream and river left.

Screw-up factor: 3-4. Swimming in this rapid is a bump-and-grind thing. The bottom of the rapid in particular gets pretty shallow. Keep your feet up.

③ Stern Squirts can be done on the eddy lines forming river right of both Pyramid Rock and Eddy 3.

Screw-up factor: 3. Flipping here in the fast water requires a reliable roll. The water is pretty deep, so make a quality attempt and you'll have time to catch the bottom of the pyramid rock eddy.

④ Teaching Eddy: Eddy Turns. Just below Pyramid Rock rapid is a nice slow section with great features for learning. It was named Teaching Eddy by whitewater instructors because it's so perfect for introducing eddy turns, peel-outs and ferries. You'll regularly see paddling classes here because the eddies are well defined and the recovery pools are large. The eddy itself, which is on river left, is so big you can't miss it. Slow-moving, deep current makes for great rolling practice.

Screw-up factor: 1. Self-rescue is easy to the right or left here.

Leaving Teaching Eddy, the river will continue straight and come back into sight of the highway. There's a rock wall on the left bank and a collection of eddies in the center of the river. These are great fun to hop through.

Downstream of the eddies on the left you'll see the gauge where the Nantahala water levels are recorded. Pull into the eddy here and check it out. (This is also a great put-in for novices.) Pay attention, though, because just around the corner the water picks up speed and gets a little challenging, bending around to the left in a long Class II stretch. After the bend, the river flows under the highway bridge and into Ferebee Park. Run under the bridge in the center of the river for the easiest line and check out the eddies on the right side for some more fun.

Delabar's Rock

 Just downstream of Ferebee Park is a fast-action rapid with a lot of fun eddies to catch. It's called Delabar's Rock.

① Easiest Routes. Enter the rapid as the main flow goes to the left side of an island and catch the eddy on the right. It is a big, long eddy, easy to catch. The conservative line is to stay in this eddy and paddle out the bottom. Follow the bend on the right side of the river, avoiding the fastest water on the left. You'll see a rock on the left that's getting hit by a lot of water and a second one downstream to the right that's splitting the current. The second one is Delabar's Rock. Your mission is to paddle between these two rocks without hitting either of them. Run this gauntlet and you're home free. Then head for the calm stretch below the rapid and eddy out left.

Screw-up factor: 3-4. The water moves around this corner faster than you might expect. Control your speed and watch for that first rock on the left. If you blow the move to the right, relax and go to the left of the first rock. There's a fun channel on the left that will plop you directly into the big left eddy..

② Eddy-hopping. More challenging is to tempt fate and catch a bunch of eddies throughout this rapid. Start in the same river right eddy and move across the current over to the small eddies along the left bank. You can eddy-hop all the way down this side and into the large eddy on the left behind the big rock jutting out from the left shore.

③ Challenging S-turn. From the eddy behind the big rock against the left shore you can see Delabar's Rock in the center of the current downstream and river right of you. The move is to exit the eddy you're in and enter the eddy behind Delabar's Rock. You'll need a fair amount of momentum to penetrate the eddy line behind Delabar's Rock, and you must time your speed appropriately. If you hit the gas too quickly, you'll be upstream of the rock, giving it a big hug. Hit the gas too late and you'll miss the eddy altogether.

Screw-up factor: 3-4. The water moves quickly here, so play it cool. If you need to self-rescue after blowing this move, carefully swim to the right.

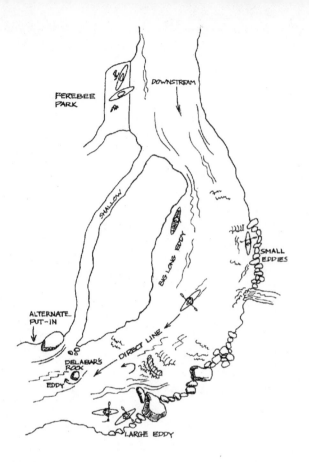

Tempting fate at Delabar's Rock

John Delabar was a schoolteacher from the Washington, DC, area who ran the whitewater paddling program at Camp Mondamin in the 1950s, '60s and '70s. A stern taskmaster who demanded absolute proficiency in paddling fundamentals from his students, John cracked up a painstakingly restored wooden canoe on Delabar's Rock. After many hours of work repairing the damage, he attempted the rapid again, only to destroy the same canoe on the same rock.

This is a fun place. After a long pool the river will take a big bend to the right. You may actually hear the quarry equipment making big rocks into small rocks to your distant river left. Take that right channel and you will see in the distance that the river hits the right bank and makes a very sharp left-hand turn. If you plan to run direct, be sure to set up this turn well, as it often sets the tone for the rest of the rapid.

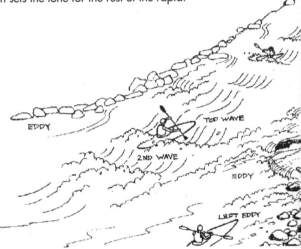

Quarry Rapid: the biggest waves on the river

1 **Direct Route.** As you go around this bend, the river straightens out and the waves build. The direct line is to round the corner on the inside of the turn near the left bank, then straighten out and hit the waves head-on, busting them wide open. Be aware of the current entering from the left; it will try to flip you to the left.

Screw-up factor: 4-5. If you flip and swim at the top, try to swim left, getting to shore above the main wave train. If you wash through the main waves, keep your feet up and ride it out, then swim left.

2 **Fun Eddies.** You can also enter this rapid by catching some fun eddies here. The first is upstream of the left bend against the right bank, under a big tree. The next one is across the current, on the inside of the bend against the left bank. This tends to be

a moving eddy and will often float you backwards around the corner. No problem; just spin your boat 180° and let the water take you around the bend, where the fun really begins.

③ Surfing. The surfer in you is going to want to spend some time here. The best access to the waves is from the left eddy just downstream of the channel that comes in on the left. Move up this eddy and look at your choices. The top wave is the fastest and the most challenging to get on. The next one down is a bit slower, easier to get on and still a fun surf.

④ Big-water Ferries. Try some big-water ferry moves and some fast-water rolls here. The eddies are small on the right side of the river but they do exist, so go for it. The water slows as you move downstream, so you can choose the level of challenge that best suits you.

Screw-up factor: 2-4. The water is deep and fast here, and you'll have a lot of time to set up and execute a good roll. Self-rescue to the left if you are at the top of the wave train. If you are halfway down the rapid or more, you can go right or left, whichever is most convenient.

Mining operations at the quarry date back to the Civil War era. In the early 1970s, the late Percy Ferebee, owner of Nantahala Talc and Lime Company, gave over 6,000 acres of the Nantahala Gorge to the people of the United States with the stipulation that the gorge remain in a wild and scenic state or revert back to his estate. The quarry was part of the same parcel of land, but will not cease to exist until 2072.

After Quarry Rapid, the river makes an S-turn through Root Canal and into Whirlpool Rapid. The water moves to the left as it enters the rapid and rebounds just upstream of a tree protuberance. Root Canal gets its name from the roots that used to stick out from the shore at this protuberance, often getting in the faces of those who floated too close to the left bank. Most of those roots have eroded away, but the water still hits the left bank hard and rebounds into the center of the river. This is a sort of mini version of the wall-shots sometimes seen on larger rivers.

① Direct Line. For a direct line, try to stay away from the left bank and run down the center of the current. As you clear the protuberance, straighten out and then hit the waves with some conviction.

② Stern Squirts and Pop-ups. You can also catch the eddy behind the protuberance for stern squirts and small pop-ups. If the water is a bit on the high side, you can get very big enders here. Recovery must be quick if you want to get back into the eddy, so roll fast or head down to Whirlpool.

Screw-up factor: 5. The stretch of river below Root Canal can be bumpy and it has some swift water. Self-rescue immediately to the left at the top. If you flip halfway down, ride it out with your feet up and swim to the right aggressively. Watch for two small rocks and the big slanting rock which form the whirlpool eddy on the left; try to stay away from these. The speed of the current and funky eddy lines make left-side self-rescue difficult. It is much easier to the right.

Hot Dogging in the Wood and Canvas Canoe Era

Long before playboats were invented, up-and-coming paddling studs had to be creative to strut their stuff. One way to do this was to run everything standing up when paddling solo. When paddling tandem, the stern paddler would stand. Another hot dog move was to stand on the gunwales while running rapids. Paddlers would train for this by canoe jousting with padded long poles on flat water. Interestingly, the thought of surfing waves never occurred to anyone, or, if it did, it never became the thing to do.

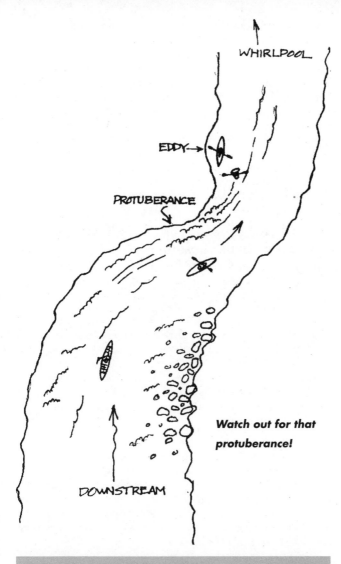

WHIRLPOOL

EDDY →

PROTUBERANCE

Watch out for that protuberance!

DOWNSTREAM

The word "Nantahala" is a corruption of the Cherokee name *Nun-daye-Li,* meaning "middle sun" or "midday sun," which refers to the fact that in places along the river the high cliffs shut out the direct light of the sun until nearly noon. The Nantahala is also known today as the "land of the noonday sun."

Whirlpool Rapid comes up so soon after Root Canal that they nearly run together. The most significant feature of Whirlpool is the large slanting rock on the river left shore. Behind this rock is the whirlpool itself, a powerful eddy with a lot of upstream speed. Across the current is another eddy, much larger and more placid than the whirlpool.

① **The Direct Line.** The direct line is straight down the center, trying not to eddy out. Sometimes, toward the bottom of this rapid the current gets confusing and changes speed unexpectedly, making it is easy to lose your balance. Keep paddling to maintain momentum and stay upright.

② **Watch the Action.** Catching the large right-side eddy is the easiest way to find a place to stop and watch the action. The current toward the top of the eddy can be strong but is not unmanageable. On a busy day you're likely to see fun tricks being performed here by squirt boaters and playboaters.

③ **Stern Squirts and Other Games.** As the water hits the slanting rock on river left it creates some interesting whirlpool effects that are fun to play games with. Once in the river left eddy behind the slanting rock you'll immediately notice its power. The current will try to force you up and into the rock at the top of the eddy. Backpaddle to maintain your position or it will be difficult to set up for your exit.

The eddy line on river left is one of the best places on the Nantahala to work on stern squirts. The move is to exit the eddy, not on the first wave but on the second wave. Try to time your stern to go under as the water is dropping from the crest of the first wave and going into the trough of the second wave. For maximum backsweep efficiency, plant your paddle deep into the eddy water to get the most purchase. Then be ready for your stern to go deep and your bow to shoot for the sky.

④ **Wave Surfing.** The wave extending out from the slant rock is fun and gives long rides. It will try to send you into the slant rock, so be prepared to bring yourself back in the other direction with good rudders and stern draws.

The swirling vortex at Whirlpool Rapid

⑤ Fun Ferries. A fun ferry is to leave the river right eddy and try to make it over to the upper river left eddy above the slant rock. Keep your angle under control and your boat up to speed and this is an effortless move. Be aware that if you blow it you can end up hitting the slant rock broadside and flip over. More than a few people have dragged their knuckles across the slant rock.

Screw-up factor: 5. Flipping in the whirlpool eddy is confusing because the current is going in so many directions. Keep your cool, be persistent and roll up. The ability to roll on both sides is helpful here but not essential. Swimming will be a challenge. It is possible to get circulated through the eddy a few times as you try to collect your gear and get to shore. If you are out of your boat downstream of the eddy, you can self-rescue to either side.

Good Put-in. A great alternate put-in is on the right in the calm water below Quarry Rapid. This put-in can be used to access Whirlpool if you just want to play there.

Blue Hole is several hundred yards below Whirlpool after a long, flat stretch. You'll notice the steep bank leading up to the road on the river right side. A nice collection of eddies here makes for some fun moves. The river makes a subtle left bend, with the water moving very fast at the top of the rapid and slowing as it moves downstream.

1 **Fast Moves in the Current.** Catch the river right eddy against the steep bank. Exit at the top of this eddy to move quickly across the current and into a very small eddy on the left bank. Also try peeling out and making an S-turn into the left eddy downstream about 20 feet. This is a fast move and very exciting.

2 **Slow Moves in the Current.** Downstream in the run-out water you will find some great eddies with slow-moving current that make for a great drill location because you can do the

VERY SMALL EDDY

LOWER LEFT EDDY

RIGHT EDDY

moves over and over. Begin in the river right eddy and ferry across into the eddy on the left bank. From here, peel out and catch the eddy behind the large rock in the center of the river. Then exit the eddy and go back to the first one on river right.

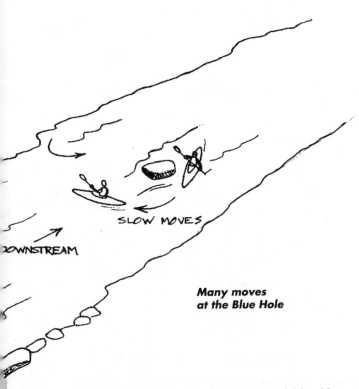

SLOW MOVES

DOWNSTREAM

**Many moves
at the Blue Hole**

Screw-up factor: 3-4. Self-rescue into the best available eddy, either right or left.

Leaving the Blue Hole, you have two options—right or left of the island. Most folks will go to the left along with the majority of the water, but try going to the right for some slow-water eddy-catching. Also notice the strangely-colored boulders here in the river. They come from the quarry.

In whitewater paddling, sometimes rapids that look like nothing offer great opportunities for playing and learning. Bunny's Eddy is one of them. You'll find it not far below Blue Hole, just below the island.

1 **Maneuver Practice.** This is an excellent place to practice crossing the current because there are such good eddies on both sides of the river. Start from the large eddy on the right and cross back and forth. You can also begin in the eddy just down-

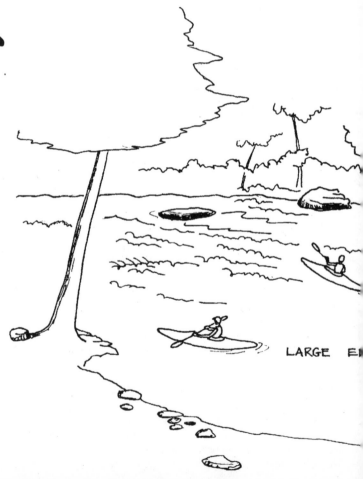

LARGE E

stream on the river left side behind a short, wide rock. Ferry back to the right side of the river. With some aggressive paddling you can make it back to the large eddy on the right.

2 **Roll Practice.** The deep water in the center is perfect for rolling practice. Exit the river right eddy and flip upstream. After successfully rolling or getting Eskimo rescued by your buddy, paddle back into the right-side eddy.

Screw-up factor: 1-2. Sometimes tree limbs get stuck between the left shore and the river left rock.

SHORT, WIDE ROCK

DOWNSTREAM →

Y

Slow water makes for great practice at Bunny's Eddy

Good Put-in. This is also one of the great put-ins on the Nantahala. The only thing that's just a little funky about it is that you have to park on the far side of the road and carry your boat across to get to the river. Cross the road very carefully and then walk upstream to find the trail to the river.

Rounding the bend below Bunny's Eddy, you will see a long, flat stretch and a rock with three humps in the center of the river.

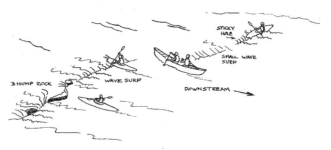

Surfing the Three Hump Rock rapid

① Wave Surf. Catch the big eddy behind this rock and look at the wave surf you have right in front of you. This wave is easy to get on but sometimes hard to stay on, and the better part of the wave lies to the river left of the hydraulic. Move out there, but pay attention—it is easy to get surfed off to river left. Keep redirecting your bow back to the river right to stay on the wave.

Screw-up factor: 3. Roll up and paddle or self-rescue into the right or left eddies.

② Side Surf. There is a sticky hole to surf coming off the river left bank. Go in there if you need to get stuck in a hole for a while. The exit is toward the river right, so you will want to enter facing the right shore, which gives you the option of paddling forward to get out. If you are facing the left bank, use backstrokes to escape.

Screw-up factor: 4. This hole can be a bit sticky and awkward for paddlers just learning about side surfs.

③ Small Wave Surf. Just to the river right of the sticky hole is another nice little surfing wave. This is a small one, but it will hold a large tandem canoe.

Screw-up factor: 2.

4 **Side Surf.** Downstream 40 yards and on the river left is a small ledge with a nice side surfing hole. You must catch the eddy just downstream and left of the side surf hole or you will miss the side surf. From this eddy, paddle into the hole and point your bow to the left bank.

Screw-up factor: **4.** It's a bit shallow here, so tuck tight and roll quickly. Self-rescue to the large eddy on the right.

5 **Roll Practice.** The deep water at the bottom of Three Hump Rock and above the Ledges is great for practicing rolls in the current.

Screw-up factor: 2-3. Although there is plenty of time to roll or self-rescue to the left here, do pay attention—the Ledges are waiting just downstream.

DOWNSTREAM

Side surfing just below Three Hump

Paddling wood and canvas canoes on the rocky streams of North Carolina demanded a level of expertise and care few paddlers have the patience for today. Most tried to use speed to control their canoes in rapids. Ferrying techniques were not used until the aluminum era when Ramone Eaton developed a more harmonious approach to river-running. Eaton found that rapids could be more efficiently negotiated by using stern ferries to move laterally and stay on the inside of bends. He became the ultimate artist-practitioner of this elegant, seemingly effortless style of paddling, and could run the entire length of Nantahala Falls without appearing to take a single stroke! Riding a high brace and using a very long paddle, he would make minute corrections to alter the boat's angle. By harnessing the current in this way, he used the river to push him exactly where he wanted to go.

Just below Three Hump is a large pool on the right. You'll also notice a picnic table pull-off up by the road. This marks the entrance to the Ledges, a challenging rapid with some fun opportunities for eddy-hopping and side surfing.

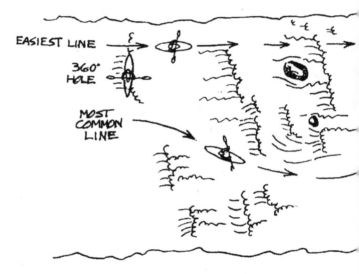

EASIEST LINE

360° HOLE

MOST COMMON LINE

The Ledges is a long, continuous, Class II rapid

1 Direct Lines. There are two direct lines through the Ledges. The easiest one is straight down the left side. Begin left and bounce over some rocks at the end or maneuver through the small channels.

The second direct line is to follow most of the water from the left at the top, moving right halfway down the rapid and then back left at the bottom. Be sure to avoid broadsiding the large rock in the main flow at river right; it can be quite dangerous if you should pin on it. The eddy to the right of the rock is often filled with debris.

2 Eddy-hopping. Eddy-hopping through the Ledges is one of the most enjoyable ways to run the rapid. There are more than 25 eddies to hit, and it's a great place to work on savvy little moves. Many of the moves are repeatable, so you can really give yourself a workout if you want.

3 **Side Surfing.** There are a number of small side surfing ledges, each with its own fun. You may even be able to pull 360s in a few of them. The smaller ledges are good for practicing hole hooks.

Screw-up factor: 5-6. The Ledges, like many rapids on the Nantahala, are fast and shallow, so if you're swimming, you should definitely assume the "safe" or "whitewater" position to avoid foot entrapment. At the top of the rapid, self-rescue quickly to the shore or to a rock in the center of the river. Remember the large rock at the bottom right and avoid broaching on that.

DOWNSTREAM

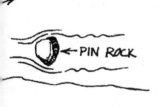

←— PIN ROCK

The next quarter-mile is fun, rolling water. The river takes a left bend and you come to "jump-off rock," a big boulder with a flat top jutting from the right bank. Stop and try it if you like. The water is deep here, but remember to always jump into a river feet-first. It is also popular to drag your boat up on the rock and plunge in, ready to paddle.

Good Put-in. A great alternate put-in lies just upstream of the Ledges. You'll know it by the roadside pull-off with a large parking area and a concrete picnic table.

The Ledges is the unfortunate location of the first drowning of a recreational boater on the Nantahala. Since the Nantahala is a fairly shallow river, putting a foot down on the riverbed in current that's more than shin deep creates significant risk of a foot entrapment—getting it caught under or between rocks and then being pushed over and held down by the current. This is what happened to the boater who drowned in the Ledges. The event was graphically reenacted in Russ Nichols's 1976 film on river safety, *Uncalculated Risk.*

45

Apple-Eater Eddy

After a long, flat pool, the river makes a right bend and an island splits about a third of the flow from the main channel. More water goes right than left before it rejoins below the island. Shortly after it merges, it passes a large, slanted rock on the left, which makes a great eddy. Directly across the river from the slant rock is another, larger eddy called Apple-Eater. The current between the two eddies is a textbook setup where you can spend volumes of time practicing fundamentals and perfecting your technique.

APPLE-EATER EDDY

1 Peel-outs. Peel-outs are best practiced from Apple-Eater. Cross out of the top of the eddy into the current, making sure to set up in a good position before you go. Recover into the bottom of the same eddy.

2 Ferries. Ferry across the current from right to left. Pay attention—the left eddy is more powerful and requires a good lean—otherwise, you're likely to flip.

3 **S-turns.** It's fun to practice graceful S-turns across the current here. Exit an eddy, cross the current and enter another eddy using as few strokes as possible.

Screw-up factor: 4. The current is deep and good for rolling, but if you want to stay at Apple-Eater for a while, don't wait too long to roll up or you'll wash past the last good eddy on the left.

DOWNSTREAM →

Surfing rapid is one of the most popular places on the river, and when you arrive there on a busy day you'll likely see plenty of other paddlers playing. As the river rounds the bend to the right, you'll see a consistent surfing wave flanked by a rocky jumble on the left and an island with a small creek running in on the right. This wave can be surfed by nearly any boat, whether it's a kayak, sit-on-top, open canoe or inflatable. You'll have access to the wave from either side, but the river left side is the most popular. Getting onto it is a bit tricky, but persistence is the key to getting it right.

Ripping the wave at Surfing Rapid

1 **Ferry Work.** Begin in the slowest current, moving upstream. The difficulty level increases as you get closer to the wave. For the most exciting ride, leave the river left eddy at the top and use the face of the wave to jet you across the river. This is a great exercise in finding your comfort level on the wave, and you can really feel the acceleration if you hit it correctly.

2 **Wave Surfing.** For access to the surfing wave from river right, first look at the water feeding into the wave very closely—there is a slight diagonal wave moving from left to right into the surfing wave. Exit the eddy at the downstream edge of the island and ferry over to the surfing wave. Do not allow your bow to dig into the hump above the diagonal wave; it is a rejector current that will push you back into the right eddy. If you place yourself strategically on this diagonal, you will catch the surfing wave nearly every time.

It's faster to get repeat attempts at the wave by accessing it from the river left side, although this is a bit trickier to learn. A small breaking wave feeds the left side and makes the entry a little more difficult. You must cross this diagonal and very strong rejector current with enough speed and angle to reach the sweet spot. The feeder wave coming in from the left is notorious for pinning your bow and pearling it down under the surface, sending you off the back and to the rear of the line.

DOWNSTREAM →

3 **Back Surfing:** Back surfing is a fun skill to practice here but the entry is the tricky part. Try spinning in the breaking wave and sliding onto the surfing wave as your stern comes around. Or line up in the eddy to get over the rejector current at the shoulder of the surfing wave. A little experimentation will find a method to get you across the rejector and onto the wave.

Screw-up factor: 2-3. The water is deep and there are good recovery eddies on both sides of the river. Watch out for the overhanging branches on the left; sometimes they have fishing line in them. Downstream and right there is a rock to duck behind if you get washed too far down. Catch the eddy here and walk up the trail back to the big river right eddy.

Good Put-in. This is also a great put-in. There is a large pull-off in the road bend, just upstream of the concrete bridge.

After rounding the corner from Surfing Rapid, you will find a straight stretch of river with great eddy-catching opportunities. One hundred fifty yards below the bend, a large eddy on river right makes a good gathering spot for large groups paddling together. A concrete bridge spans the river just downstream.

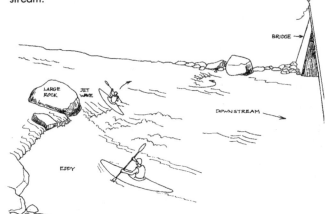

Setting up for the jet move at Fast Ferry

1 Eddy-catching above the Bridge. Just upstream of the bridge a large rock on river right creates a deep, wide eddy. The water rebounding off the rock makes a fast eddy line with a wicked rejector current. Maintain a piercing angle to the eddy line and carry a lot of speed to penetrate deep into the eddy. If you know someone is following you closely, move deep into the eddy and allow them full access to the eddy line—you may spare yourself a bruised kidney.

Screw-up factor: 3. Deep water makes for a good place to roll, and both banks are suitable for self-rescue.

2 Jet Move. The wave at the top of the eddy near the rock is a fun one to jet out onto. Maintain your speed and a conservative angle as you cross the eddy line, exiting on the face of the wave and moving over to the river left eddy above the rock.

Screw-up factor: 3. If you flip, roll quickly to make it back into the bottom of the eddy on river right.

3 **Good Surfing below the Bridge.** Fifty yards below the bridge, the water is channeled to the river right and forms two waves. One is obvious, the other is not so obvious.

The first wave you see can be surfed, though the rides are typically short. Try catching the small eddy (1) upstream and left of the wave to stop your downstream speed, then ferry over to the wave.

Screw-up factor: 2-3. Flipping upstream of the rock can cause some anxiety, but stay calm if you can and take the split second you need to do a quality roll.

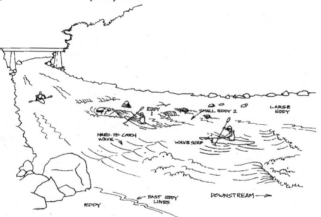

Fun moves below the bridge

4 **More Wave Surfing.** Just upstream of the rock splitting the current is a small wave that is easy to overlook. It's a great wave with easy access. Move up the very large eddy on river left and behind the small eddy (2) above it. Look at the water very closely and notice the small mound forming upstream and just river left of the wave. Take this rejector current into account as you move onto the wave below the mound.

Screw-up factor: 2-3. If you're sent off the river right side of the wave there is a slim chance you could end up hitting the rock. Once past the rock there's flat water suitable for good rolling.

Good Put-in. Below the concrete bridge on the right there's a wide, flat spot above the Chamber of Waves. Look for a nice pull-off with a concrete picnic table.

Below the wide, flat pool an island splits the river. The left channel is shallow and filled with overhanging branches, making the right channel the preferred route.

1 Rolling Waves. In the right channel there are some nice rolling waves—great fun for the novice boater. Be sure to go around the boulders at the top by heading right or left of center and then moving back to the center when you have cleared them. Try floating through sideways and practice balancing the boat as it rocks with the waves. Keep your hips loose and rock with the water.

Screw-up factor: 2-3. The water is fast and creates a foot entrapment potential, so if you find yourself swimming through here, keep your feet at the surface and make for either shore. Watch for branches on the left.

2 Wave Surf. A nice surfing wave lies in the center about halfway down the rapid. Catch the eddy on river left for moderate-to-easy access, or turn and face upstream, breaking your downstream speed with forward strokes. This wave will give long rides if you catch it cleanly.

Screw-up factor: 2-3. Downstream of the wave, keep an eye out for the rock on the right. Catch the eddy behind it for a view of your friends coming downstream.

Upper Gorgarama

The Chamber of Waves enters directly onto the mad, swirling vortex of barbecue, boiled peanuts and souvenir shops known as Gorgarama.

3 Textbook Eddy. This eddy is located directly under the barbecue stand and is a great place to practice peel-outs. The eddy line is very clean, the current is slow enough to allow repeated attempts, and a novice can make errors without being hammered by the current. If you make the right noises and roll over a few times the diners above may even throw you some scraps. Seal noises typically work best.

Screw-up factor: 1. This is an outstanding learning spot.

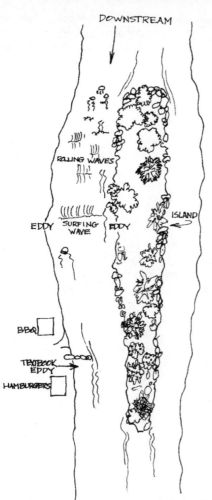

DOWNSTREAM

ROLLING WAVES

EDDY   SURFING WAVE   EDDY   ISLAND

BBQ

TEXTBOOK EDDY

HAMBURGERS

Through the Chamber of Waves and into BBQ land

Early paddlers on the Nantahala—mostly summer campers—did not wear lifejackets. Camp leaders believed lifejackets were unsafe and that wearing one would keep a swimmer in a hydraulic, preventing him from going deep enough to catch the current leaving the hole and continuing downstream. Some campers did not begin wearing PFDs until the 1970s or early '80s. Today, of course, wearing a lifejacket on the Nantahala is required by law.

Moving downstream and around the right bend in the river brings you through a flat shoal of a rapid where an island once again splits the river. Wildwater racers trying to speed down the river in record time will choose the left channel because it cuts the corner well. Most folks choose the right side, where you can find some fun eddies to catch and a small hole to surf.

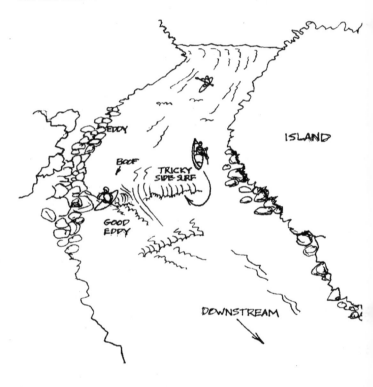

AKA:

Little S.O.B.

Going for the boof in Gorgarama Shoals

① Fun Lines. Catch the eddy on river right above the two small ledges and choose some fun lines in and out of the three or four eddies.

Screw-up factor: 3. Flipping here may wash you down onto some shallow rocks. If you do flip, tuck tight and take the time for a quality roll.

2 **Boof.** The first ledge is good for a small boof that lands you right in the eddy next to the river right shore. Begin in the eddy above the boof rock. A few strokes for speed, with some right angle while timing the last stroke on the left, will land you squarely in the eddy below it.

Screw-up factor: 1-2. It's no problem if you miss the boof. Just catch the eddy or continue downstream.

LEFT
CHANNEL

3 **Tricky Side Surf.** The first ledge has a small pour-over that makes a steep and sometimes tricky surf. Use the left side for a smoother ride and prepare to use a lot of lean if you get too far right. The best way to enter this hole from its river left side is to catch the eddy behind the hole and paddle in pointed toward river left. 360s can be done on that left side of the hole.

Screw-up factor: 4-5. The entry into this hole is steep, making for a deceptively sticky ride. You may get surfed a while if you flip over; try to exit either side of the hole if you want out.

The Great Smoky Mountain Railway has been in operation since 1988 as a scenic railroad. Trips originate in Bryson City and run regularly through the Nantahala Gorge, bringing 200–300 people twice daily during the tourist season.

Just downstream of the Gorgarama section a swinging bridge crosses the river. Well upstream of the bridge there's a fun rapid with a good surfing wave and a combination of eddies to catch.

LARGE BOULDER

SURFING WAVE

SMALL BOULDER

The moves upstream of the Swinging Bridge

① S-turn/Wave Surf Move. Begin on the left side of the river in an eddy behind the large boulder. Peel out from there and look for the small boulder in the center of the river. S-turn through that eddy from left to right, leaving the eddy with some angle pointed upstream. Ferry over to a small surfing wave 10 yards to the river right of the eddy. If you miss the eddy or the wave, just turn downstream and keep moving. You'll improve your chances of making this move by controlling your downstream speed before entering the S-turn, then ferrying to the wave under control.

Screw-up factor: 3-4. The water is shallow.

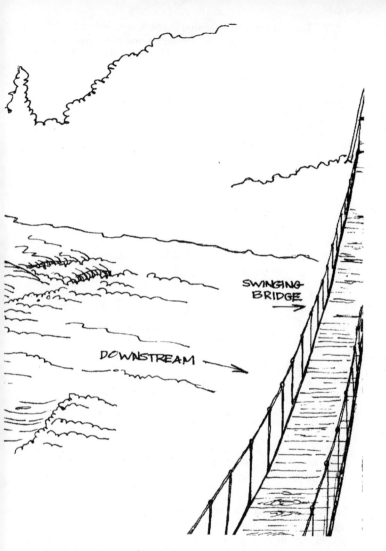

SWINGING
BRIDGE →

DOWNSTREAM →

2 **Fun Eddy Turns.** Look for good eddies underneath the swinging bridge. Their crisp and forgiving eddy lines make catching them a fun way to slow down and regroup before heading downstream.

Screw-up factor: 2. If you swim, self-rescue to the right. Sometimes there are trees caught in the rocks under the bridge.

Below the swinging bridge the river turns left and is filled with some boulders that make for one of the most enjoyable little rapids on the river. A large eddy on river left just above the turn has a great eddy line and is a good place to begin with a group. Around the corner there are two rocks in the left center of the river with fun eddies to catch behind them. Against the right bank is another good eddy and downstream of this one are two more, one on either side of the current. These five features account for the name of this stretch of river.

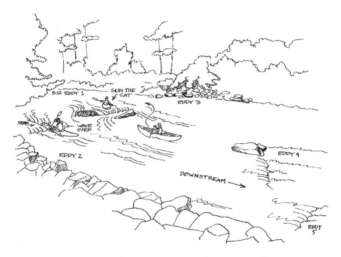

Skinning the cat in Five Eddy Rapid

1 **Easy Line.** The easy line is to run river right all the way through the rapid, rounding the corner on the inside near the river right bank.

Screw-up factor: 4. Self-rescue right or into the eddy in the center of the river. The water stays deep in the main channel but gets shallow in some places.

2 **Eddy-hopping.** It's fun to eddy-hop through this rapid, making up ferries and attainment moves. If you're paddling with a group, practice eddy-hop scouting, an important skill you'll need for paddling more difficult rivers.

Screw-up factor: 4.

3 **Skin the Cat.** To make this hot little move, leave the river left eddy and sneak in between the rocks, making a quick S-turn and ending up in the large eddy in the center of the river.

Screw-up factor: 5. It is easy to get caught on the second rock. If you blow it, lean toward the rock and you won't have a problem getting around it. If you flip here, roll with good form and you should come right up.

4 **Wave Surf.** The wave in the center of the current is accessible from eddies on either side. It will try to push you into the left eddy, but you can maintain the surf with some strategic stroke work.

Screw-up factor: 4. Sometimes, flipping in here will wash you downstream quickly, so roll and head back into the eddies or continue downstream.

5 **Attainments.** You can also do some fun attainments here. Move back upstream on the river left side of the rapid. Cross below the skin-the-cat rocks, skin the cat in reverse, and then continue across above the rocks for even more challenge.

Screw-up factor: 3. Some branches hang down into the water on river left. Keep your paddle low to avoid snagging them.

Early in the 1970s, a small group of experienced decked boaters was making a winter descent. As they headed into Five Eddy Rapid, the lead paddler pulled into the first big eddy on the right and came face to face with a mule standing chest deep in the river. It wore a halter, and a lead line tied to a long board was tangled in its legs, preventing it from climbing out of the river and up the steep bank. As soon as the paddlers freed the mule's head, it happily scrambled up the bank out of the cold water. When the group walked the mule down the road to the Nantahala Outdoor Center, they were told a local farmer had stopped by the previous day looking for his mule. It seems the mule had somehow either kicked or fallen out of the back of his truck!

This is the final rapid before Nantahala Falls. You'll run a small rapid known as Donny Dutton with a picnic area on the right just before entering the Bump. In this rapid, look for fun eddies to catch, a great attainment opportunity, and a good-sized pour-over hole.

1 **Easiest Lines.** There are two conservative routes to keep you away from that crashing pour-over hole at the bottom left that gives the rapid its name.

Leaving the large eddy at the inside corner far above the Bump itself, run down the extreme right side of the rapid. Go right of the large boulder and catch some of the big eddy behind it. This will make it easier to stay to the right side as you pass the hole.

For a little faster ride, run just left of the same large boulder without getting pushed to the left too far. Once you are past the bump hole, go anywhere you want.

Screw-up factor: 5. The water moves swiftly here. DO NOT stand up or attempt to walk to shore. Foot entrapment risk is high. Swim with your body flat on the surface and go for either shore.

2 **Eddy-hopping.** There are a number of eddies to catch through this rapid, beginning at the top against the right bank. Keep your downstream speed under control from the top and move through as many as you feel comfortable with. The eddies on the left above the bump hole are the fastest and most challenging.

Screw-up factor: 5. In the event you miss an eddy on the left and go through the bump hole unexpectedly, try to straighten out and hit it perpendicular with some speed to pop right through. Hit the hole sideways and you may get tipped over but not recirculated; the water crashes through the hole but will not keep you. Stay tucked until you roll.

3 **Boof Op.** The boof opportunity is downstream and on the far left, off the boulder just upstream of the pour-over hole. Boof off the right side of the rock, using a combination right stroke and thrust to land your boat flat in the eddy. If you hit this just right you will get that characteristic boof landing noise when your hull hits the water.

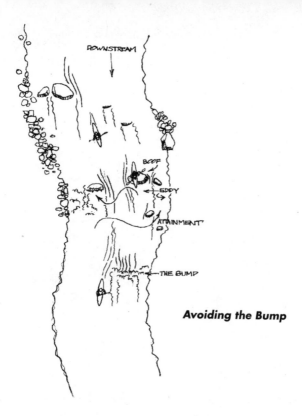

DOWNSTREAM

BOOF

←EDDY

ATTAINMENT

THE BUMP

Avoiding the Bump

Screw-up factor: 4-5. If you flip, relax and roll up—you have more time than you realize before going over the Bump. Be ready to paddle through it when you come up. A quick roll may allow you to stay in that eddy you and gravity teamed up to get into.

4 **Attainments.** Catch the left eddy via boof or determined eddy turn. S-turn out of the left eddy and into the eddy center. From here you can attain back into the left eddy, making your move just upstream of the Bump hole. This can be a gut-check, but controlled boat angle and good forward strokes make it truly attainable.

Screw-up factor: 4-5. The pour-over is right behind this move. If you blow it, run the Bump straight on.

Nantahala Falls

When someone tells a story about running the Nantahala River, the first question always asked is, "How was your run at the Falls?" It's no wonder. This Class III rapid is exciting for the novice as well as for the developing rodeo boater. Complete with grandstands on the river right shore and overflow car parking, this is the place to be on a summer afternoon.

Nantahala Falls: so much to do, so little time!

Scouting the Falls. There are some important features in this rapid to use as reference points when scouting and also while you are in the rapid. Find these on the illustration: Billboard Rock, the island, the small pour-over below the Island, Truck Stop Eddy, Micro and Macroeddy, the Top Hole and the Bottom Hole. Also check out the recovery eddies on both sides of the river.

1 Standard Route. The route most popular for novices is to run left of the island, staying in the main flow of water past Billboard Rock, left of the small pour-over and into Truck Stop Eddy. Enter Truck Stop with some speed and determination directly through the roostertail waves near the top of the eddy. Grab hold of some real estate on that left bank to hold your position in the eddy while you scout your line through the main drop. You can move downstream while still in this eddy to get a better look.

From the bottom of Truck Stop you can paddle to the left of the Top Hole and punch through the Bottom Hole into good eddies on either side of the river. When you get to the Top Hole you have two choices: follow the green-water tongue to the right and through the V, or aim left and run through the Bottom Hole head on. Many folks lose it in the Bottom Hole, failing to go far enough right and hitting it sideways. If you recognize in time that you will not make the move to the right, turn your boat angle back to the left so you are perpendicular to the hole and can punch cleanly through.

Screw-up factor: 6. The fast water above the Falls can cause flips and a long swim. Swimming aggressively, you can often get to shore before going through the main drop. If you do swim through the main drop, pull your knees toward your chest and roll into a ball to avoid the possibility of foot entrapment. Once you are through the Bottom Hole, move to the right-side eddy, where there is likely to be a rope-thrower. Whew.

2 **Eddy-hopping.** The eddies throughout the Falls area are plentiful. Start at Billboard Rock or check out the eddy above Billboard for more excitement. The eddy river center of Billboard Rock is a difficult ferry away and an even more difficult ferry back. There are small eddies down the left side and one on the right at the base of the island, and more still across from Truck Stop Eddy on river right.

Screw-up factor: 6. The water is fast through this section and can be intimidating, but it's plenty deep for rolling. If you swim, go for either bank aggressively to get out of the water above the main drop. Let go of your gear if absolutely necessary, but if you can, bring it to shore with you.

It is not known who made the first descent of Nantahala Falls, but we do know about the first women who ran it. According to Aurelia Kennedy, Pat Bell (daughter of Frank Bell), who ran it in 1953 with Ramone Eaton, was the first. Aurelia was the second. Then 19 and a canoeing counselor at Camp Merrie-Woode, she paddled the Falls during the summer of 1954 in a tandem wood and canvas canoe. That September, Aurelia married Payson Kennedy. In 1972, along with Horace Holden, Sr., Aurelia and Payson founded the Nantahala Outdoor Center.

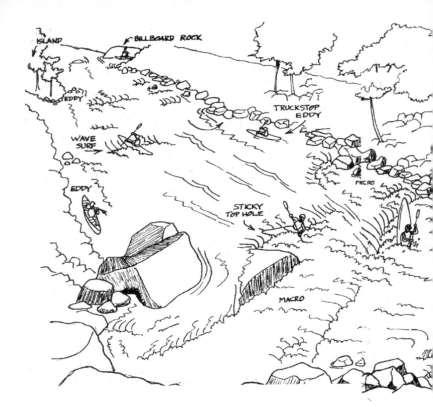

3 **Micro to Macro Moves.** Begin in the last eddy on river right above the main drop and slowly ferry over to Microeddy. Enter Micro with your boat angled upstream. If you try to enter with downstream angle and downstream speed it is easy to puncture the eddy and ram into the left bank, which will send you into a tailspin and over the bottom drop backwards. This first move into Microeddy requires a delicate balance of angle and speed control. The next move, into Macroeddy, requires power and angle control. Leave Micro and cross the eddy created by the Top Hole without turning too much to river right, which would turn your boat upstream. Use powerful strokes to cross the eddy line and enter Macroeddy aggressively.

Screw-up factor: 6. Be prepared to run the main drop of the Falls backwards if you blow this move. If you swim, it's no big deal; the deep water below the drop is great for rolling. Self-rescue to the right if necessary.

4 **Wave Surf.** There is a nice wave in the current about 20 yards upstream of the main drop. It has great access eddies on both sides (the one on the left is Truck Stop). The river right side crashes a little and the left is more smooth. The wave tends to surf you into Truck Stop Eddy, so to get the best surf you should try to redirect back toward the crashing part of the wave.

Screw-up factor: 5. Remember that the main drop of Nantahala Falls is directly downstream of this wave.

5 **Rodeo Moves.** Enders, pirouettes and cartwheels can all be done in the Bottom Hole. The best access is from the eddy on river left, though you must cross up and over the pesky little ledge with a sticky hole to reach it. The sweet spot in the pourover is just where the water turns solid green and is no longer transparent.

Screw-up factor: 6. A good roll is essential if you want to have fun playing here. "Three-second Rock" is downstream of the main drop. If you flip in this hole, you have three seconds to make a roll before hitting the rock. If your attempt takes longer, stay tucked so you'll wash over it instead.

This stretch begins at the base of Nantahala Falls and extends to any of the take-outs at NOC. This section of river has many fun moves, surfing waves and even a few small play holes. It's a great stretch to do when taking a new boat out for a short demo run.

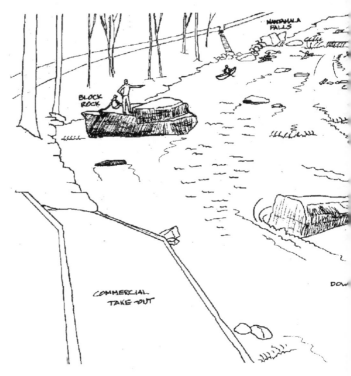

The action below the Falls

1 **Hole Surf.** In the left center of the river is a small hole perfect for hole-riding practice. Find it 50 yards upstream of the first take-out on the right and across from the large block rock on the right. The eddy in the backwash makes a good coaching spot if you're paddling with a novice boater. You can float in your boat or stand in the waist-deep water, giving assistance when it is needed.

Screw-up factor: 4. This hole can be sticky when you want to exit. Work to the edges to get out, and tuck if you flip.

2 **Wave Surf.** Downstream of the block rock and hole is another large rock with a big eddy and a small wave forming off its left corner. This is an excellent small wave to learn on. It's also a good place to practice back surfing.

Screw-up factor: 1. The water is quite calm around this wave, the water is deep for rolling and the eddy behind the big rock makes a nice recovery spot.

3 **Attainments.** It is possible to begin at NOC and attain all the way up to the Falls for an ender session. This is a great way to get in a workout if you're short on time. There are a few moves that might require a little thought and more than one attempt. Keep trying and you will get it. I could tell you the secret to making all the moves, but then there would be no mystery left for you.

Screw-up factor: 2.

The Falls-to-NOC stretch is a popular set of rapids for boaters who are interested in purchasing a new boat and would like to try it out on whitewater before buying. Local outfitters have demo boats available for the prospective buyer to try. Someone adept at attainment moves can put in and take out near the NOC footbridge and get in a pretty good paddle. It's a great way to decide which boat is right for you.

This slalom training site has been used by slalom racers for as long as the Nantahala has been paddled, and is filled with great river features that allow boaters to develop a number of skills. Check the sidebar for an explanation of slalom rules and gate use.

Working out in the gates

① Direct Line. The easiest line through here is to follow the main current around the island to the right and through the wave. Below the wave the water channellizes and moves toward the left side of the river; continue to the left and into the take-out eddy.

Screw-up factor: 3. Don't forget that Greater Wesser Falls is 100 yards downstream of the river left take-out eddy. Don't miss this eddy. If you swim, self-rescue to the left aggressively.

② Slalom Training. Slalom rules state that red gates are upstream gates and green ones are run in the downstream direction. You'll notice that none of the gates here have colors. These are practice gates that can be slid around on their wires into different positions for endless combinations of tricky moves. In a race, a series of gates is set up to be run in a timed event. Two seconds are added to a racer's time for touching a gate, and fifty seconds are added for missing one completely.

Screw-up factor: 4. The water is fast here and flips happen. Begin in the slowest water at the bottom of the rapid and gradually move upstream to increase the difficulty.

3 **Wave Surfing.** The wave in the center of the current just upstream of the bridge is an awesome surfing wave. Access is available from eddies on both sides, but the easiest entry is from river right.

Screw-up factor: 4. The water is moving fast through this wave. Recover into big eddies on the right or left directly under the bridge. The take-out is on the left if you swim that way.

4 **Cartwheels.** Directly downstream of the point of the island is a small rock with a pour-over on the river right side, perfect for cartwheels in very small rodeo-style boats.

Screw-up factor: 2. Roll up and get back up there.

Slalom athletes can often be found training in this section of river. You'll recognize them by their boats, since racers are nearly the only whitewater paddlers who use a boat over ten feet long any more. Slalom boats are four meters in length and are constructed of high-tech composite fibers and laminated plastics. They are designed to be sleek and fast. Compared to a playboat, slalom boats are less stable and more difficult to turn.

Whitewater canoe and kayak slalom racing is very similar to slalom skiing. Racers negotiate a series of 25 gates in numerical order through a boulder-strewn rapids course. Upstream gates have red poles and racers enter them paddling upstream. Downstream gates have green poles and are run in the downstream direction. Penalties are added to a paddler's time if gates are missed or touched. (A gate run in the wrong direction is treated as a missed gate.) Fifty seconds are added to the time for each miss. Two seconds are added for each touch. There are four Olympic slalom classes:

Men's Kayak – K1
Men's Canoe – C1
Men's Tandem Canoe – C2
Women's Kayak – K1W

The Tuckaseigee River Rapids

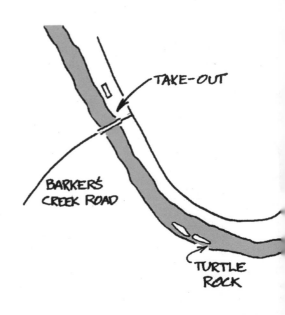

TAKE-OUT

BARKER'S CREEK ROAD

TURTLE ROCK

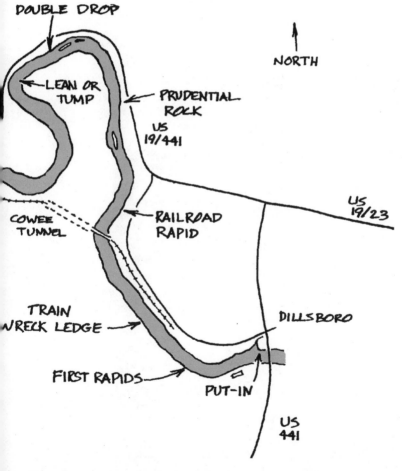

DOUBLE DROP

LEAN OR TUMP

PRUDENTIAL ROCK

US 19/441

NORTH

COWEE TUNNEL

RAILROAD RAPID

US 19/23

TRAIN WRECK LEDGE

DILLSBORO

FIRST RAPIDS

PUT-IN

US 441

The put-in is at the park in Dillsboro at the confluence of Scotts Creek and the Tuckaseigee River.

Once you find the put-in and get situated to begin your river trip, don't be in a hurry to head downstream immediately because there are some great warm-up spots right here. The large pool where you put in is a nice place to do some stretches and warm-up rolls. Paddle up the creek to the first corner and there are even some easy eddy lines to play around with. The water is shallow in the creekbed, so go out near the main river current where it is deeper to do warm-up rolls.

Tuckaseigee Put-in

1 **Good Eddy Line.** Where the river current meets the mouth of the creek you'll find an easy eddy line for working on peel-out techniques. The large eddy makes a safe place to work on this skill.

2 **Midstream Ferries.** Straight out in the center of the river you'll see four islands in a diagonal row angling upstream toward the bank. These are the pilings of an old bridge and they make a good ferry practice spot in slow and gentle water.

Screw-up factor: 1. The current is slow here, but a little shallow.

Starting your day on the Tuck

SCOTT'S CREEK

The first rapid on the Tuck is a small Class I rapid with many eddies and a very straightforward direct route.

1 **Direct Line.** Begin in the center and move left as you get to the bottom. Some maneuvering is necessary to get around shallow rocks, but it is all pretty easy; just follow the main channel of water. Try not to get too far left to avoid getting tangled in the overhanging tree limbs.

2 **Eddy-hopping.** Catch the first eddy on the right at the very top. From here you can see the rest of the rapid and plan your course through the many eddies below.

3 **Wave Surf.** There is a small wave at the bottom of the first rapid on the left. You can get to the wave from the eddy on the left bank 20 yards below the overhanging tree limbs. It is a small wave, perfect for learning to shred, so go for it.

Screw-up factor: 2. The current is a little faster here, but not so very fast. Self-rescue either side or to large shallow eddies

4 **Peel-outs & Ferries.** 100 yards below the bottom of the first rapid, the river makes a small right bend. Against the left bank there is a good eddy with a very nice eddy line, which is a great place to work on peel-out skills. Use the two culverts on the bank (one is big, one is little) as landmarks to find the eddy line. The current is slow enough to cross without too much difficulty and awesome for learning to do ferries.

Screw-up factor: 1. The current in the center is deep and you can self-rescue to either side.

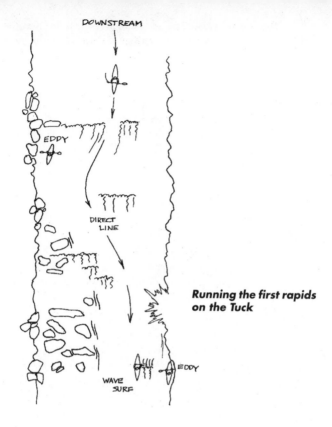

Running the first rapids on the Tuck

The second rapid is just downstream of a power line crossing the river. You may also see the old gauge on the left bank. Here, there are two rocks with great eddies behind them. Use these eddies to practice ferries in slightly faster water.

1 Wave Surf. There is a small wave surf to the river left of the ferry place. Use the large eddy on river left to rest between surfs.

Screw-up factor: 2. The water is plenty deep to roll in the fast current. Self-rescue to either shore or to the big eddy in the middle.

Train Wreck Ledge is several hundred yards downstream of the second rapid. Just upstream of the ledge, some great boulders in the river make nice eddies to use for slow-water eddy turns. The water is pretty deep in some spots and good for rolling practice. Be sure to check the depth before you flip as there are boulders just below the surface in places.

On river right is the train yard for the Great Smoky Mountain Railway, an excursion train used for sightseeing in the Tuck Gorge. Just downstream of the train yard is the site of the train wreck scene in the movie *The Fugitive*. The wreck is still there.

1 The Direct Routes. There are two direct lines through Train Wreck Ledge. The first is down the left side and is shallow and rocky—a very conservative line.

The other direct route is on river right, where all of the water is going around the ledge. It's an S-turn series of moves where you begin by dodging the shallow rocks above the ledge, move right around or through the hole at the end of the ledge, and then back to the left in the main flow river left of a boulder.

2 In-and-Out Eddy Turns. Catch the large eddy behind the ledge. It can be entered from either side of the river. From the eddy behind the ledge, set up to peel out to river right and catch the eddy behind the boulder about ten feet off the river right bank.

Screw-up factor: 2. Watch for the little ledge hydraulic on the river right side. It's easy to avoid—just don't drop in sideways.

The Cowee Tunnel, which cuts through the mountain between Railroad Rapid and Lean or Tump Rapid, is supposedly haunted. Legend has it that in 1883 when the group of 20 convicts building the tunnel was attempting to ferry across the rain-swollen river, their boat capsized. The men wore shackles and were chained together. Of the 20, only one man survived, and the ghosts of the 19 who drowned inhabit the tunnel to this day.

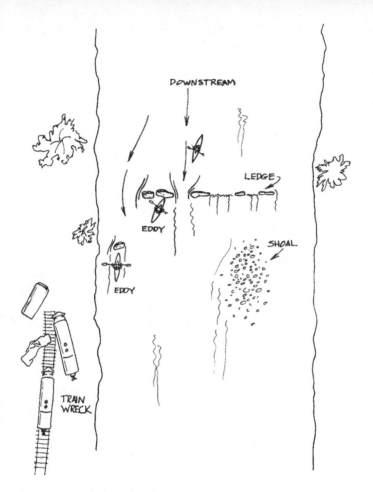

In-and-out eddies of Train Wreck Ledge

In 1993, Hollywood came to the Tuckaseigee Gorge to make *The Fugitive*, starring Harrison Ford. The first full-scale train wreck to be captured on film was shot on the river right bank, just downstream of Train Wreck Ledge. You can view the remaining wreckage as you paddle by, but do obey the no trespassing signs and stay in your boat. The movie includes a superb overhead view of the wreckage and the river as the search for the fugitive begins.

After a long, shallow stretch that parallels a campground on the left, the river flattens and makes a right bend. When you see a railroad bridge crossing the river, you'll know you're at Railroad Rapid. This rapid is broken into upper and lower sections by a flat pool.

Upper Railroad

1 **Direct Line.** There are two direct lines through Upper Railroad. The right side offers the most conservative route, which runs straight through the shallow water, bumping over some rocks. The other direct line begins on the left, following most of the flow. You'll see the current turn back to the right and into the pool above Lower Railroad. This S-turn route is easy to see.

2 **Eddy-catching.** Catch the eddy behind the bridge pilings for a good look downstream before entering the rapid. From here you can see a number of eddies to catch as you make your way through the rapid.

Screw-up factor: 3. This is fairly shallow and bouncy water and you'll need to watch for strainers along the river left shore.

Lower Railroad Rapid

1 **Direct Line.** The direct line is down the right side, punching through the hole at the bottom. You can avoid the hole altogether by running just left of it and catching the eddy downstream and to the left.

2 **More Eddy-catching.** The slow water above the drop allows plenty of time to look things over and get up some speed to punch through the hole.

The left-side eddy is behind the large slab rock sitting in the center of the river. From the slow water above, get some right-to-left momentum going to punch into that eddy.

The right-side eddy is a little trickier to catch because the large boulder jutting out from the shore can be a little intimidating. For this one, get some momentum going from left to right and hit that eddy high to avoid colliding with the rock. If you do hit the rock and flip, relax and roll up or swim around it. The big eddy at the bottom right is a good place to regroup.

Screw-up factor: 3. Be sure to hit the hole with momentum or you will flip! The water is deep here so a roll should not be a problem.

③ Pop-ups and Back Enders. The steep hole on the river right edge has a pour-over that can be good for doing pop-ups. For front enders, move up the river left eddy and then ferry over to the eddy formed by the hole. Feel around with your bow for the sweet spot, then put in a good forward stroke to drive your bow in for the pop-up. Typically, back enders work a little better, but these take some comfort-level surfing time in the hole to maneuver your boat for the setup. For the back ender, side surf with your bow facing the river right bank. As your bow leaves the hole and turns downstream, use a backstroke to engage your stern for some big air. Smaller rodeo boats tend to get both back and front enders better and more easily.

Screw-up factor: 4. Watch out for the large boulder downstream and river right of the back ender hole.

BIG
EDDY

Back endering in Lower Railroad

Prudential Rock

From the bottom of Railroad Rapid the river is split by an island; you can run down either side. After the island there are a few hundred yards of slow-moving water and many eddies before you come to the biggest rapid so far, called Prudential Rock. The name comes from the large, dark-colored rock on the river right. Most of the water is going into Prudential Rock. It is not difficult to see how it got its name, because many paddlers have gotten a piece of it. The large round-top rock to the left of Prudential is called Spaceship Rock. It gets its name from its extra-terrestrial appearance at certain water levels.

Going for the moves at "The Rock"

① Direct Line. To take the direct line, run between Spaceship and Prudential rocks, angling left. In the center of the current just left of Prudential Rock is a crashing wave. It is not difficult to go left and miss the wave altogether if you choose. It's also fun to line up on that wave and crash right through it. Eddy out left below Spaceship or continue in the main flow and head downstream to the large eddy on the left in front of the sandy beach.

Screw-up factor: 4. If you drift too far right, you could get a piece of the rock—maybe more than you want. Be sure to hit the crashing wave with plenty of speed to avoid a flip. The water is good and deep here, so a roll should not be a problem.

(2) Hot Move. If you're feeling particularly spry and you want to go for a difficult move, catch the eddy behind Spaceship Rock. From behind Spaceship, cross over and into the eddy in front of Prudential Rock. From here you can go back to the Spaceship Rock eddy or continue around Prudential to the right.

Screw-up factor: 6. If you blow this, you could pin.

(3) Eddy Turns, Peel-outs, S-turns, Roll Practice. At the bottom of Prudential Rock rapid is a large eddy on river left in front of a large sandy beach, known as **Teaching Eddy**. There is another eddy on the river right side directly across from the sandy beach eddy. This piece of current is one of the best places anywhere to work on basic skills.

Screw-up factor: 0. Go for it. The lack of consequences here is what makes it such a good teaching eddy.

Lower Teaching Eddy. From the sandy beach teaching eddy continue downstream several hundred yards through some slow-moving water with some easy and fun eddies to catch. As you begin to see the river bending to the left, there will be two large boulders near the river right bank where all of the current is going. These two boulders form some very nice eddies that also make excellent spots for boat-handling work.

Screw-up factor: 0. The water here is plenty deep and slow, making it another great learning spot.

U-Haul Rapid. Looking up the right bank as you leave Lower Teaching Eddy, you'll see the U-Haul rental place, which is the tip-off that you are about to enter U-Haul Rapid. Run this rapid on the river left side—you'll find many eddies to catch at the top. The river right side becomes increasingly shallow as you head toward the bottom of the rapid and all of the water gets channeled into a wave train running along the river left bank. The large rock sticking out from the left bank has a great eddy behind it. Be sure to use proper form and a good lean when you catch it because this eddy turn can be very dynamic.

Screw-up factor: 2. The water is shallow here and there are a lot of boulders. Do your best to stay upright.

After U-Haul Rapid the river moves slowly for about half a mile to a left bend where the riverbank is very steep and filled with blasted boulders. As you get to the bend there will be some very nice eddies to catch in slow-moving water. Just past it, you'll see the horizon line for Double Drop Rapid.

You guessed it, this rapid has two drops to it. Neither are very large or technically demanding, but they do produce some large waves and a fun eddy to catch, which gives this rapid a sort of big-water feel. Eddy out left or right at the bottom.

Dropping in on Double Drop

1 **Direct Line.** The direct line goes right down the middle. It is incredibly fun to line up at the top in the center of the current and paddle as fast as you can, hitting the waves straight on and busting them wide open

Screw-up factor: 1. If you flip at the top and exit your boat, keep your feet up and swim for either eddy—right or left—at the bottom of the rapid.

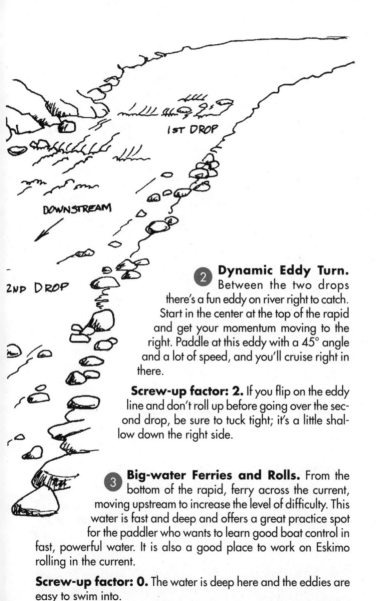

1ST DROP

DOWNSTREAM

2ND DROP

② Dynamic Eddy Turn. Between the two drops there's a fun eddy on river right to catch. Start in the center at the top of the rapid and get your momentum moving to the right. Paddle at this eddy with a 45° angle and a lot of speed, and you'll cruise right in there.

Screw-up factor: 2. If you flip on the eddy line and don't roll up before going over the second drop, be sure to tuck tight; it's a little shallow down the right side.

③ Big-water Ferries and Rolls. From the bottom of the rapid, ferry across the current, moving upstream to increase the level of difficulty. This water is fast and deep and offers a great practice spot for the paddler who wants to learn good boat control in fast, powerful water. It is also a good place to work on Eskimo rolling in the current.

Screw-up factor: 0. The water is deep here and the eddies are easy to swim into.

83

Just below Double Drop Rapid is Lean or Tump Rapid, easily recognized by the large rock extending from the left bank. The main flow goes to the right of this rock.

LARGE EDDY

EDDY LINE

DOWNSTREAM

Negotiating the tricky eddy line at Lean or Tump

1 **The Direct Line.** To run direct, just follow the main flow as it goes around the rock and continues downstream.

Screw-up factor: 1. There are a few rocks to watch out for, but you can easily see these when boat scouting in the slow water above the rapid.

2 **Eddies to Catch.** The rapid gets its name from the large eddy on the left with a very well defined eddy line. If you

EDDY

attempt to enter this eddy without adequate lean, you will "tump" over. Cross into the eddy with your boat perpendicular to the eddy line and leaning to the left. Be sure to hold that lean until you have stopped turning completely and you will be in without problems. If you do flip, don't sweat it—you'll be in a deep eddy with lots of time to roll.

There is another eddy against the river right bank that makes a challenging ferry destination from the left eddy. Hold your angle as you cross the current, keep your speed up and you'll get there just fine.

Screw-up factor: 1. The water is deep for good rolling if you have to.

The last significant rapid of the run is Turtle Rock. Nearly a half a mile downstream from Lean or Tump after a long, flat stretch, it is just past the large gray house on river left and is part of the right-hand bend. The large boulder in the center of the river with green moss on the top is known as Turtle Rock.

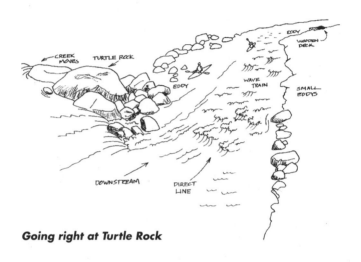

Going right at Turtle Rock

1 **Direct Line.** Begin heading to the right bank after you see the large gray house. Stay to the inside of the right bend and to the right of Turtle Rock. The water will funnel down into a wave train. Catch the large eddy on the right below the wooden deck.

Screw-up factor: 1. Be sure to line up near the right bank as you enter this rapid to get the best of the wave train below.

2 **Eddy-catching.** After entering the wave train, catch the eddy to the left. From here you can cross the current into the very small eddies against the right bank. The farther downstream you make these moves, the easier they become.

Screw-up factor: 1. The water is a little fast, but plenty deep.

③ Creek Moves. Over to the left of Turtle Rock you will see a narrow channel with very minimal flow and some fun eddies to catch. The moves are tight and technical but the water is moving slowly, so they are not too difficult.

Screw-up factor: 2. Good boat scouting through this section will help you to avoid any mishaps.

 From here to the take-out is mostly Class I with a few shallow rapids. Pay attention to keep from sticking or broaching on rocks.

The take-out is underneath the bridge on the river right side at Tuckaseegee Outfitters. These folks allow boaters to take out on the premises as a courtesy. Return the favor and treat the property with respect—no littering, of course, and be sure not to block the take-out with your shuttle vehicle.

It is not known who made the first whitewater descent of the Tuckaseigee Gorge, but it may well have been Frank Bell, who paddled the river in the 1930s, before the building of Fontana Dam. A whitewater canoeing pioneer, Bell made many first descents of popular rivers in western North Carolina.

Alternate Put-ins:
On the Nantahala

Because US 19/74 runs alongside the river, many alternate put-ins are available to help you design your paddling day. Parking at these put-ins may not always be an option, so plan to drop off your boats and run a shuttle.

Big Eddy below Patton's Run

7.6 miles upstream of the NOC Outfitters Store. The large eddy just below Patton's Run is the perfect put-in if you want to avoid the first big rapid. Pull off at the overlook on Highway 19 above Patton's Run. From the downstream side of the parking area, follow the trail to the river.

Power Line Put-in

7 miles upstream of the NOC Outfitters Store. Pull off under the power lines and follow the trail down to the put-in. This is an especially good put-in for large groups.

Teaching Eddy Put-in

5.8 miles upstream of the NOC Outfitters Store. This put-in allows access to the river right side at Teaching Eddy. Park across the road.

Gauging Station Put-in

5.5 miles upstream of the NOC Outfitters Store. Use it when the put-in at Ferebee Park is super busy. The slow water makes it a good place for novices to warm up before heading downstream.

Ferebee Park

5.2 miles upstream of the NOC Outfitters Store. An extremely popular place to put in, with a large grassy area nice for stretching and warming up. On cold days it's often drenched with warm sunshine. You can usually park here unless it's very busy.

Whirlpool

4.8 miles above the NOC Outfitters Store. Look for a pull-off with a concrete picnic table. The trail to the river is steep and often slippery, but leads to a section of slow, wide flatwater. Paddle upstream to Whirlpool for destination playboating.

Bunny's Eddy

4.4 miles upstream of the NOC Outfitters Store. The parking spot is on the left-hand side of the road. Getting to the put-in is a little tricky because you must carry your boat across the road to get to the river. The put-in trail is upstream of the parking spot and is a little steep, so watch your step.

The Ledges

3.5 miles upstream of the NOC. A pull-off with a concrete picnic table marks the put-in for the Ledges. You'll be putting on the river between Three Hump Rock Rapid and the entrance to the Ledges.

Surfing Rapid

2.4 miles upstream of the NOC Outfitters Store. Pull off on the right. This put-in will give you direct access to one of the best surfing waves on the river. It's also a put-in for the last two miles of river, ending at Nantahala Falls.

Sampler Eddy

2.1 miles above the NOC Outfitters Store. Put in at the picnic table pull-off. The name of this eddy comes from the "sampler stretch" of river, a 1.2-mile section with a number of Class I and II rapids that begins here and ends at Donnie Dutton Park. Sampler Eddy is large and the current here is slow. It's a great place to begin and to work on easy ferries.

Donnie Dutton Park

0.9 miles upstream of the NOC Outfitters Store. Most often used as a take-out for folks not wanting to run Nantahala Falls, this place has a nice beach with a big eddy. It is also used by families for picnicking, so don't plan to park here all day. If you want to warm up a little before heading down to play in the Falls, this is definitely the starting place for you.

Nantahala River Sections

This page of river sections is the result of many years teaching canoeing and kayaking on the Nantahala. Use it when you're looking for stretches of river appropriate for yourself or a group of paddlers, based on the skill level and learning goals of the paddlers. It's also useful if you or your group have limited time to spend on the river and running the entire Nantahala is not an option. There are many put-in and take-out combinations (see pps. 88–89). Here are four of the most popular options.

Sampler Eddy to Donnie Dutton Park

Commonly referred to as the "Sampler Stretch," this short run is approximately 1.2 miles in length and takes about an hour to paddle. The Sampler Stretch is an easy section with mostly Class I and a few Class II rapids. Many paddlers get their very first taste of whitewater on this section of the Nantahala.

Teaching Eddy to Surfing Rapid

This is a 3.4-mile, approximately four-hour section which takes you down the middle portion of the river. Consisting mostly of Class II rapids and a lot of them, it's a great stretch for paddlers who want to practice running rapids without the pressures of negotiating Patton's Run and the Falls. For an even shorter option, you can take out at the Ledges.

Surfing Rapid to NOC

This is a 2.4-mile stretch that can be paddled in anywhere from one to four hours, depending on how much playing you do. Commonly known to the locals as "Surfin' Down," this section is a good one if you want to begin by shredding your brains out at Surfing Rapid and finish the day with enders at the Falls.

Above the Falls to NOC

Choose this stretch if you want to spend your time playing at Nantahala Falls. The top of the rapid is a great warm-up with many eddies and a fun wave to surf, but the main attraction is the bottom hole at the main drop. This is where you can really practice your rodeo stuff.

AWA Rapids Classification
(American Whitewater Affiliation)

Class I: Easy. Fast-moving water with riffles and small waves. Few obstructions, all obvious and easily missed with little training. Risk to swimmers is slight; self-rescue is easy.

Class II: Novice. Straightforward rapids with wide, clear channels which are evident without scouting. Occasional maneuvering may be required, but rocks and medium-sized waves are easily missed by trained paddlers. Swimmers are seldom injured and group assistance, while helpful, is seldom needed.

Class III: Intermediate. Rapids with moderate, irregular waves which may be difficult to avoid and which can swamp an open canoe. Complex maneuvers in fast current and good boat control in tight passages or around ledges are often required; large waves and strainers may be present but are easily avoided. Strong eddies and powerful currents can be found, particularly on large-volume rivers. Scouting is advisable for inexperienced parties. Injuries while swimming are rare; self-rescue is usually easy but group assistance may be required to avoid long swims.

Class IV: Advanced. Intense, powerful but predictable rapids requiring precise boat-handling in turbulent water. Depending on the character of the river, it may feature large, unavoidable waves and holes or constricted passages demanding fast maneuvers under pressure. A fast, reliable eddy turn may be needed to initiate maneuvers, scout rapids, or rest. Rapids may require "must" moves above dangerous hazards. Scouting may be necessary the first time down. Risk of injury to swimmers is moderate to high, and water conditions make self-rescue difficult. Group assistance for rescue is often essential but requires practiced skills. A strong Eskimo roll is highly recommended.

Class V: Expert. Extremely long, obstructed or very violent rapids which expose a paddler to added risk. Drops may contain large, unavoidable waves and holes or steep, congested chutes with complex, demanding routes. Rapids may continue for long distances between pools, demanding a high level of fitness. What eddies exist may be small, turbulent or difficult to reach. At the high end of the scale, several of these factors may be combined. Scouting is recommended but may be difficult. Swims are dangerous, and rescue is often difficult even for experts. A very reliable Eskimo roll, proper equipment, extensive experience and practiced rescue skills are essential.

Class VI: Extreme and Exploratory. These runs have almost never been attempted and often exemplify the extremes of difficulty, unpredictability and danger. The consequences of errors may be severe and rescue may be impossible. For teams of experts only, at favorable water levels, after close personal inspection and taking all precautions.

Glossary

360. Surfing a boat full circle (360°) in a hole, while remaining in the hole.

Access eddy. An eddy from which a play spot (a wave or hole) can be entered. Good play spots have good access eddies.

Angle. Refers to the angle the boat makes to the current. A "piercing angle" is one where the boat is perpendicular to an eddy line. A "conservative," "safe" or "closed" angle is one where the boat is at less than a 45° angle to the current. A "radical" or "open" angle has the boat at a greater than 45° angle to the current.

Attainment. The act of paddling a boat upstream using a series of eddies. Enter the backwash of an eddy, paddle up to the base of the obstruction that creates it, and ferry into the backwash of the next upstream eddy.

Back surf. Surfing with your stern in the upstream direction.

Big air. Describes an ender that shoots the boat and paddler completely out of the water.

Boat scouting. A method of scouting a rapid that allows you to ease up to the top of or ferry above a rapid to look at it without getting out of the boat.

Boof. A technique used to land a boat flat at the base of a vertical drop. The name comes from the sound the boat hull makes on impact.

Broaching. Pinning a boat perpendicular to the flow of the current. The obstruction is typically a rock or tree limb and is often a dangerous place to be, but broaching is also sometimes used intentionally as a boat scouting technique.

Cartwheel. The linking of bow and stern whippets for a 360° spin perpendicular to the surface of the water. Think of the boater's body as an airplane with the boat being the propeller.

cfs. Cubic feet per second. A means of measuring the flow rate of rivers.

Crashing wave. A surging wave that builds and then crashes into a temporary hole.

Destination boating. Paddling in a specific rapid and taking out there without going downstream, for the purpose of using the whitewater features of that one rapid.

Downstream speed. Refers to the rate at which a boat and paddler move downstream. Downstream speed can be controlled by using river features like eddies and waves and the current itself to eddy-hop, wave surf and ferry.

Dynamic. Describes a whitewater move that is fast, forceful, and/ or intense.

Eddy. The calm water behind an obstruction to the current, such as a rock or log.

Eddy-hop. To move from eddy to eddy through a rapid. Used for boat scouting and for creating more difficult moves within rapids.

Eddy line. The line created where moving current meets the edge of an eddy.

Eddy turn. A technique used to cross out of the current and enter an eddy. This is a fundamental skill necessary to paddle under control through a rapid.

Elevator move. A dynamic attainment.

Ender. Submerging one end of the boat in the current so that the other end shoots into the air in the vertical plane and lands end over end. Bow enders submerge the bow, shooting the stern into the air. Back enders sink the stern and shoot the bow into the air.

Escape. The place where an exit to a hole exists. Often it is current flowing past the hole at its edge, or the water flowing beneath it. Also, the action of exiting a hole: to escape it.

Flat spin. A 360° spin performed in a hole or on a wave.

Front surf. Surfing a wave with the bow pointed in the upstream direction.

Green water. The non-aerated water feeding into a wave or hole.

Hairy ferry. A ferry move which crosses the current directly above a hazardous river feature.

Hole. A steep wave, often at the bottom of a drop, that crashes into an upstream recirculating current. Holes come in all sizes and levels of difficulty to play in; some holes are best to stay out of. Also called a "hydraulic."

Hole hook. Slapping a hole with the front portion of the boat to stop downstream momentum and begin a hole surf.

Linking ends. See Cartwheel.

McTwist. A whippet done at 45° or less.

Microeddy. A very small eddy.

Mystery move. A move that results in complete submersion of the boat and paddler. Typically done in a squirt boat, but sometimes done inadvertently in surface boats.

Pearling. The shallow submersion of one end of the boat by the current, often unintentionally, during a surf or ferry. (The aerated water creates a "pearly" visual effect.) Pearling your bow usually has a detrimental effect on your intended move.

Peel-out. A technique for exiting an eddy and entering the current under control.

Pillow. A cushion of water formed on the upstream side of an obstruction, sometimes surfable.

Pirouette. An ender incorporating a more-or-less 360° spin done in the vertical plane.

Pop–up. Submerging one end of the boat in the current so that the other end shoots into the air at less than a 90° angle to the surface.

Protuberance. A part or thing that protrudes.

Rejector. A wave or current that pushes you away from your intended destination.

Recovery eddy. An eddy used after playing in a wave or hole to prevent the boater from washing downstream.

Retentive move. A stunt performed in a hole that lands the boat and paddler back in the hole.

Retro move. A playboating move that has withstood the test of time.

River left. To the left, facing downstream.

River right. To the right, facing downstream.

Self-rescue. The act of recovering yourself and all of your equipment in the event of a swim.

Side surf. Typically done in a hole with the boat perpendicular to the current or parallel to the hole.

Shred. To have complete control and confidence in your boat while performing playboating stunts with style and panache.

Slap the hole. To allow the front of the boat to hit the hole broadside, changing the direction of a surf or slowing the boat.

Splat. A squirt move in which the elevated bow or stern of the boat comes to rest against a rock or other obstruction, momentarily pinning the boat against the obstruction. In essence, a controlled pin.

Squirt. Using the current to submerge one end of the boat in order to elevate the other end. Bow squirts sink the bow and elevate the stern. Stern squirts sink the stern and elevate the bow.

Standing waves. A series of tall waves, similar to a wave train.

Stunts. Playboating tricks like 360° spins, cartwheels, whippets and stern squirts.

Surface boats. Most playboats are paddled on the water's surface and are thus called surface boats. Squirt boats are paddled subsurface and do not fall into the surface category; just about any other boat does.

Surfing. The act of riding a hole or shredding a wave.

Wall shot. A term to describe strong whitewater current hitting a rock wall or riverbank at any angle, creating a pillow and then rebounding back into the main current. Sometimes you can play on the pillow, but often wall shots are best left alone.

Wave. A wave is caused by water moving over an obstruction—a rock, for example. Waves are also formed when water is compressed as it moves through a narrower channel. The speed of the water forming the wave, the height of its crest and the steepness of its face combine to make each wave unique.

Wave train. A series of standing waves in a line.

Whippet. A move in which one end of the boat is submerged in a hole and the other end moves 180° through a nearly vertical plane, landing the boat and paddler back in the hole. It's actually the first half of a cartwheel and it differs from an ender in that the motion is from side to side rather than end over end.

Wildwater. Another name for whitewater. Also a name for downriver sprint racing. Wildwater boats are designed for straight-line speed and have small "wings" that jut out behind the cockpit.

Bibliography and Suggested Reading

For more information on the origins of playboating and histories of paddling on the Nantahala and Tuckaseigee rivers, the following are recommended:

The Squirt Book by James E. Snyder. Menasha Ridge Press, Birmingham, Alabama. 1987.

Canoeing Whitewater: A Guidebook by Randy Carter. Appalachian Outfitters, Oakton, Virginia. 1967.

"River Exploration in the Southern Appalachians" by Payson Kennedy. In *First Descents,* edited by Cameron O'Connor and John Lazenby. Menasha Ridge Press, Birmingham, Alabama. 1988.

Also by Kelly Fischer

A Playboater's Guide to the Ocoee River. Milestone Press, Almond, North Carolina. 1997.